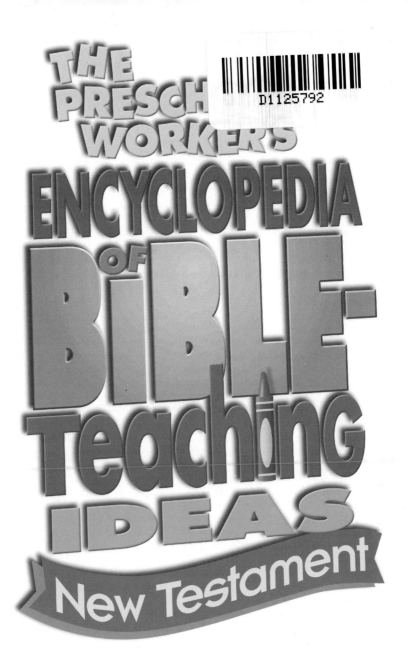

THE PRESCHOOL WORKER'S ENCYCLOPEDIA OF BIBLE-Teaching IDEAS

New Testament

Group
Loveland, Colorado

Group's R.E.A.L. Guarantee to you:

Every Group resource incorporates our R.E.A.L. approach to ministry— a unique philosophy that results in long-term retention and life transformation. It's ministry that's:

This is EARL.
He's R.E.A.L.
mixed up.
(Get it?)

Relational
Because student-to-student interaction enhances learning and builds Christian friendships.

Experiential
Because what students experience sticks with them up to 9 times longer than what they simply hear or read.

Applicable
Because the aim of Christian education is to be both hearers and doers of the Word.

Learner-based
Because students learn more and retain it longer when the process is designed according to how they learn best.

The Preschool Worker's Encyclopedia of Bible-Teaching Ideas: New Testament

Copyright © 2001 Group Publishing, Inc.

Visit our Web site: **www.grouppublishing.com**

Credits
Contributing Authors: Donna Alexander, Michelle Anthony, Jacqui Baker, Tim Baker, Karl D. Bastian, Glynis Belec, Chip Borgstadt, Katy Borgstadt, Delphine Boswell, Herbert Brokering, Jody Brolsma, Carolyn Caufman, Jane McBride Choate, Karen Choi, Robin Christy, Joy B. Cole, Laurie Copley, Mary Ann Craven, Ruthie Daniels, Mary Davis, Karen Dockrey, Melissa Downey, Kathy Duggan, Jacqui Dunham, Lisa Flinn, Nanette Goings, Debbie Gowensmith, Lisa Graben, Jerayne Gray-Reneberg, Sheila Halasz, LaDona L. Hein, Karen B. Humphrey, Ellen Javernick, Lois M. Keffer, Ken Kellner, Cindy Kenney, Jan Kershner, Mary J. Kurth, Julie Lavender, Leanne Leak, Nancy Lettardy, Morey Levenson, Susan L. Lingo, Janice Long, Carol Mader, Pamela Malloy, Kelly Martin, Christina Medina, Julie Meiklejohn, Janet Miller, Sherry Miller, Rev. Mike Morris, Barbie Murphy, Cynthia Nelson, Nancy Nelson, Cindy J. Newell, Ken Niles, Lori Haynes Niles, Jennifer Nystrom, Anna Page, Leticia Parks, Stephen Parolini, Nancy Paulson, Cindy Peppers, Ray Peppers, Lois Putnam, Siv M. Ricketts, Beth Rowland, Liz Shockey, Donna Simcoe, Carol Smith, Cindy Smith, Linda Stephan, Bonnie Temple, Debbie Thompson, Dave Thornton, Martha Turman, Helen Turnbull, Mary Van Aalsburg, Joyce Whitehead-Elliot, and Jennifer Root Wilger
Editors: Laurie Copley and Linda Anderson
Senior Editor: Karl Leuthauser
Chief Creative Officer: Joani Schultz
Copy Editor: Dena Twinem
Art Director: Kari K. Monson
Computer Graphic Artist: Joyce Douglas
Illustrators: Amy Bryant and Dana Regan
Cover Art Director: Jeff Storm
Cover Designer: Alan Furst Inc.
Production Manager: Peggy Naylor

Unless otherwise noted, Scripture taken from the HOLY BIBLE, NEW INTERNATIONAL VERSION®. Copyright © 1973, 1978, 1984 by International Bible Society. Used by permission of Zondervan Publishing House. All rights reserved.

Library of Congress Cataloging-in-Publication Data
The preschool worker's encyclopedia of Bible teaching ideas : New Testament.
    p. cm.
  Includes index.
  ISBN 0-7644-2295-2 (alk. paper)
    1. Bible–Study and teaching (Preschool) 2. Christian education of preschool children.
I. Group Publishing.

BS2530 .P74 2001
268'.432–dc21

                                                                                    2001023296

10 9 8 7 6 5 4 3 2 1   10 09 08 07 06 05 04 03 02 01

Printed in the United States of America.

CONTENTS

INTRODUCTION 5

   Matthew..7

   Mark..27

   Luke 49

   John...75

   Acts...95

   Romans 105

   1 Corinthians..115

   2 Corinthians..121

   Galatians 129

   Ephesians 133

   Philippians..137

   Colossians 141

   1 Thessalonians 145

   2 Thessalonians 149

   1 Timothy...151

   2 Timothy...155

   Titus 159

   Philemon 161

   Hebrews 163

   James 169

   1 Peter..175

   2 Peter..179

   1 John...183

   2 John...187

   3 John...189

   Jude 191

   Revelation 193

SCRIPTURE INDEX 200

TEACHING-STYLE INDEX 202

THEME INDEX 204

Ask:

• **Why do you think the wise men brought gifts to Jesus?**

• **What kind of gifts can we give to Jesus?**

Say: **Today we're going to make spicy sachets to remind us of the gifts the wise men brought to Jesus and that we can give gifts to Jesus to show him we love him.**

Have children move to the craft area and decorate their envelopes with stickers and colorful crayon scribbles. Give each child three cotton balls. Have children hold the cotton balls while you put a couple of drops of vanilla or cinnamon oil on them. Have children slide the cotton balls inside the envelopes, then lick the adhesive flaps and seal the envelopes.

MATTHEW 3:16-17

THEME:

God wants us to please him.

SUMMARY:

Use this affirmation idea to teach children that affirming others is pleasing to God.

PREPARATION:

You'll need a Bible and a feather.

Have children sit in a circle. Open your Bible to Matthew 3:16-17, show children the passage, and read it aloud. Say: **This means that when Jesus was baptized, the Holy Spirit came down to earth, and God said that he was pleased with his Son, Jesus. To be pleased with someone means to be happy with that person.**

Ask:

• **What are things Jesus did that pleased God?**

• **What are things we do that please God?**

Say: **Today we are going to tell some things that please us about our friends. I'll blow the feather. When it lands on someone, I'll tell one thing about that person that has made me happy. Then the person who the feather landed on will blow the feather to someone else and tell something that has made him or her happy about that person. We'll play until everyone has had the feather.**

You may need to prompt less verbal children. After each child has had a turn, close in prayer asking God to help all of us be the kind of people who please him.

MATTHEW 4:18-22

THEME:

We can follow Jesus.

SUMMARY:

Use this finger play to teach children about Jesus calling the disciples.

PREPARATION:

You'll need a Bible.

Open your Bible to Matthew 4:18-22 and show children the passage. Say: **Jesus wanted people to follow him and help him teach about God's love. They were called disciples. This passage tells about Jesus calling his disciples to follow him. Let's learn a rhyme about the story.**

Have the children repeat the phrases and do the corresponding actions with you.

Jesus walked along the shore. *(Walk two fingers of right hand along left forearm.)*

He watched *(put right hand on brow to shade eyes)*

The boats at sea. *(Touch the fingers of both hands together to form a triangle boat, and rock them back and forth.)*

He loved *(put both hands over heart)*

The busy fishermen. *(Pretend to use a fishing pole.)*

He called *(cup hands around mouth)*,

"Come follow me." *(Beckon with hands.)*

Ask:

• **Why do you think the disciples followed Jesus?**

• **What can we do to show Jesus that we'll follow him too?**

• **How does that make Jesus feel when we follow him?**

Close in prayer asking Jesus to help us follow him each and every day.

MATTHEW 5:16

THEME:

Shine your light for Jesus.

SUMMARY:

Use this service idea to teach children to share their love of Jesus with others.

PREPARATION:

You'll need a Bible, old crayons, small containers, a blanket, a flashlight, candle wicking and small

PREPARATION:

You'll need a Bible.

Have the children form a circle and sit down. Open your Bible to Matthew 19:19b, show children the passage, and read it aloud. Say: **In this passage, Jesus tells us to love others as we love ourselves.**

Lead the children in repeating the verse with you. Ask:

• **What do you think it means to love your neighbor as yourself?**

• **Who are your neighbors?**

• **What are things we can do to show our neighbors we love them?**

Say: **Pick one of your neighbors sitting next to you to be your partner. Tell your partner one kind thing you like people to do for you.**

Pause and let the children share their answers.

Say: **Now pretend to do the kind act for your partner.**

Ask:

• **How do you think your neighbor felt when you did your kind act for them?**

• **What kind things can you do for people who live near you?**

Lead children in the following closing prayer:

Help us, God, to love our neighbors and do what is right.

When we show our love to others, we're sharing Jesus' light. Amen.

MATTHEW 21:6-11

THEME:

We can praise Jesus.

SUMMARY:

Use this celebration party to teach children about Jesus' triumphal entry into Jerusalem.

PREPARATION:

You'll need a Bible, confetti, newsprint, crayons, markers, stickers, scissors, canned vanilla frosting, rainbow candy sprinkles, and plastic knives. You'll also need ready-to-bake sugar cookie dough and craft sticks to make a celebration wand cookie for each child.

Prepare the cookies before class by slicing the cookie dough according to package directions. Before baking them, insert a craft stick into each cookie and follow the baking directions.

As children enter your room, cheer for them and say: **Hooray, [name] is here!** Add children to the cheering section as they arrive. Give children confetti to throw over children as they enter the room. When everyone has arrived, gather children together, and ask:

• **What surprised you when you arrived today?**

• **How did you feel having people cheer for you?**

• **What was it like to cheer for your friends?**

Say: **Today we're going to have a party to celebrate and cheer for Jesus.**

Give each child a 2½-foot length of newsprint with the long sides folded to the middle (see illustration). Have children decorate their coats with markers, crayons, and stickers. As they're working, cut necklines and arm holes in each child's coat. When finished, have children wear their coats and sit in a circle. Say: **One day Jesus came to a city called Jerusalem. Many people crowded around and cheered for Jesus.**

Open your Bible to Matthew 21:6-11, show children the passage, and read it aloud. Ask:

• **Why do you think the people put their coats on the ground?**

• **Would you want to put your coat on the ground for Jesus?**

Say: **Putting coats on the ground was one way the people showed they knew Jesus was special. Let's show Jesus we think he's special.**

Have children pretend that Jesus is coming into the room. Have children take off their coats, lay them on the ground, and shout the praise words used in the passage. Say: **"Hosanna to the Son of David! Blessed is he who comes in the name of the Lord! Hosanna in the highest!"**

Ask:

• **How did you feel when you put your coat on the ground?**

• **What are other ways we can show Jesus we think he's special?**

Give each child a celebration wand cookie. Have children spread frosting on their cookies using plastic knives, then decorate with the rainbow sprinkles. Have children carefully wave their celebration wands and shout: **Hosanna in the highest! Jesus is special!** Then have children enjoy their snack.

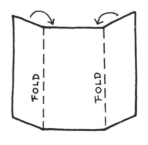

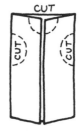

Mark

"He said to them, 'Let the little children come to me, and do not hinder them, for the kingdom of God belongs to such as these.' "

Mark 10:14b

MARK 1:3

THEME:

We can prepare our hearts for Jesus.

SUMMARY:

Use this object lesson to teach children that we can straighten the road for Jesus to get ready for his coming.

PREPARATION:

You'll need a Bible and a long rope.

Before the activity, make a path in your room with a long rope. Put lots of bends, twists, and curves in the path.

Have the children take off their shoes and walk on the "tightrope." When the first child is several feet along the path, have the next child begin. After everyone has walked the path, straighten the rope, and have the children walk along the path again. Then gather the children and ask:

• **Was it easier to walk along the crooked path or the straight path? Why?**

Say: **The Bible talks about making a crooked path straight. Let's read what it says.**

Open your Bible to Mark 1:3, show children the passage, and read it aloud. Say: **To straighten the road for Jesus means to get ready for his coming. We can get ready for Jesus by looking at our lives and by getting rid of the things that keep us from following Jesus.** Ask:

• **How can we welcome Jesus in our hearts?**

• **How does Jesus feel when we welcome him into our hearts?**

Close with a prayer asking God for help in preparing our hearts for Jesus.

MARK 1:12-13

THEME:

We must worship God only.

SUMMARY:

Use this song to teach children that we can turn to God when we're tempted, so we worship only him.

PREPARATION:

You'll need a Bible.

Have children sit in a circle on the floor. Open your Bible to Mark

MARK 10:13-16

THEME:
You are important to Jesus.

SUMMARY:
Use this affirmation activity to teach children that Jesus loves them.

PREPARATION:
You'll need a Bible.

Open your Bible to Mark 10:13-16, show children the passage, and read it aloud. Say: **Jesus was sad that the disciples tried to send the children away, because he loved the children and wanted to see them.**

Ask:

• **How do you think the children felt when the disciples tried to send them away?**

• **How do you think the children felt knowing that Jesus wanted to see them because he loved them?**

• **How do you feel knowing that Jesus loves you?**

Say: **Let's learn a fun rhyme to help us remember that we're important to Jesus and that he loves us, too.**

Say the following rhyme to children and do the motions. Encourage children to join in with you as they learn the words. On the fourth line, call a child's name and have him or her come sit in your lap. Repeat the rhyme until each child has had a turn.

The disciples said, "Stay back. *(Shake finger back and forth.)*
Jesus is a very busy man." *(Hold hand in front of you.)*
Jesus said, "Come close, for I have a special plan. *(Speak in a gentle voice and beckon.)*
Come [child's name]**, sit upon my knee** *(have child sit in your lap),*
For you are important to me." *(Give child a hug.)*

MARK 10:46-52

THEME:
Jesus does many miracles.

SUMMARY:
Use this creative storytelling idea to teach children about Jesus healing a blind man.

PREPARATION:
You'll need a Bible.

Have children sit in a circle. Say: **I want all of you to close your eyes and keep them closed until I tell you to open them.**

Ask:

- **What do you see?**
- **How does that feel?**

Have children open their eyes. Open your Bible to Mark 10:46-52, and show children the passage. Say: **This is the story of Jesus healing a blind man. Just like when we closed our eyes and couldn't see, this man couldn't see at all even with his eyes open. As I tell the story, I need you to help me act out the motions.**

There was a man very long ago *(put your hands on your hips),*

His friends all called him Bart. *(Give your neighbor a high five.)*

He begged all day in Jericho. *(Cup your hands in front of you.)*

It was enough to break your heart. *(Shake your head sadly.)*

You see, poor Bart was blind as could be. *(Point to your eyes.)*

He couldn't see at all. *(Put your hands over your eyes.)*

But a man was coming who could make the blind see! *(Point down the road.)*

Bart started to shout and call! *(Cup your hands around your mouth.)*

Bart yelled out, "Have mercy on me!" *(Stretch out your arms in front of you.)*

And Jesus stopped to say *(walk in place, then stop),*

"Your faith is strong. I'll make you see." *(Pretend to look through binoculars.)*

Bart's eyes were healed right away! *(Clap your hands.)*

But old Bart's story didn't end right there. *(Shake your head "no.")*

That's not what the Bible says. *(Hold your hands like an open book.)*

For Bart found that Jesus really cares *(put your hands over your heart),*

So he followed him all of his days. *(Walk in place.)*

Ask:

- **How do you think Bart felt when Jesus healed his eyes and he could see? Why?**
- **Why do you think that Jesus healed Bart?**
- **How do you think it made Jesus feel to heal Bart?**

Say: **Jesus cared for Bart and loved him. He cares for us and loves us, too.**

Close in prayer, thanking Jesus for his miracles and for his love.

MARK 12:28-31

THEME:

We can love God and our neighbors.

SUMMARY:

Use this song to teach children that God commands us to love him with our whole hearts, and to love our neighbors.

PREPARATION:

You'll need a Bible.

O pen your Bible to Mark 12:28-31, show children the passage, and read it aloud. Say: **This passage tells us about the two greatest commandments we are to follow. Commandments are special rules we must obey. The two greatest commandments are to love God with all our heart, all our soul, all our mind, and all our strength, and to love our neighbor as we love ourselves.**

Ask:

• **How can we love God with all our heart, soul, mind, and strength?**

• **How can we love our neighbor as we love ourselves?**

• **How does God feel when we** follow his commandments?

Say: **Let's learn a song to help us remember God's commandments.** Teach children the words to this song sung to the tune of "Clementine." Have children hold hands and skip around the circle to the right on the first verse, then switch directions and skip to the left on the second verse.

Love God, love God,
That is what I am to do.
When I love God, I please him,
And it makes me happy too.

Love my neighbor, love my neighbor,
That is what I am to do.
When I show love to my neighbor,
It makes God so happy too.

MARK 14:32-42

THEME:

Jesus wants us to pray.

SUMMARY:

Use this prayer to teach children about Jesus praying in the Garden of Gethsemane.

PREPARATION:

You'll need a Bible.

Open your Bible to Mark 14:32-42, and show children the passage. Say: **This passage tells about the time that Jesus prayed for himself and for others while he was in the Garden of Gethsemane. We can pray for ourselves and for others just as Jesus did.**

Have the children form a line. Choose a child to help you form a bridge. Say: **I want you to think of some things you can pray for as we begin to march under the bridge.**

Sing this song to the tune of "London Bridge":

> **God will listen when you pray,**
> **When you pray, when you pray.**
> **God will listen when you pray.**
> **What will you say?**

Drop the bridge, and capture a child. Ask the child to name something or someone you can pray about together. Say a sentence prayer with the child and then raise the bridge and start the song over again. Continue until everyone has a chance to be captured and to pray. Then have children sit in a circle, and ask:

• **Why does God listen when we pray?**

• **How does God feel when we pray?**

Close in prayer thanking God for listening to us whenever we pray.

MARK 14:66-72

THEME:

Jesus wants us to forgive others.

SUMMARY:

Use this game to teach children about Peter disowning Jesus.

PREPARATION:

You'll need a Bible.

Have children sit in a circle on the floor. Let each child tell about one of his or her friends. After everyone has had a turn, say: **Let's play a game called Friendship Tag. I'll call out something, and you must tag someone who fits what I said. For example, if I say, "Tag someone wearing blue," find someone with blue on and tag that person.** Call out clothing colors, hair colors, names, or physical characteristics.

Afterward, have children sit back

in the circle and say: **Jesus loves you. He's your friend. Jesus had a special friend named Peter. They liked to spend time together. But one day, Peter said Jesus wasn't his friend. This made Jesus very sad.**

Open your Bible to Mark 14:66-72, show children the passage, and paraphrase the story. Ask:

• **Have you ever made a friend sad?**

• **What did you do?**

Say: **Peter made a bad choice when he said he didn't know Jesus. That made Jesus sad, but he forgave Peter. Jesus wants us to forgive our friends, too, when they hurt our feelings. Let's practice telling our friends that we're sorry and ask for forgiveness.**

Form pairs. Have partners pretend they've been fighting over a toy. Then have them apologize and ask for forgiveness. Close in prayer thanking God that he forgives us, and ask him to help us forgive those who hurt us.

MARK 15:33-39

THEME:

Jesus died for us.

SUMMARY:

Use this music activity to teach children that we can express sorrow for Jesus' death and joy for his resurrection.

PREPARATION:

You'll need a Bible and a variety of rhythm instruments such as tambourines, rhythm sticks, and sand blocks. If such instruments are unavailable, use pots and pans, sticks, sandpaper glued to wood blocks, and jingle bells.

Gather children, and say: **We make music to express the way we feel. Sometimes our music is happy. But when we're sad, we make music that sounds sad too.**

Open your Bible to Mark 15:33-39, show children the passage, and tell a paraphrase of the story. Ask:

• **Why did Jesus die?**

• **How do you think Jesus' disciples felt when he died? Why?**

• **How does Jesus' death make you feel? Why?**

Say: **Let's make sad music with**

these rhythm instruments to remind us how Jesus' disciples must have felt that day.

Ask:

• What do you think sad music might sound like?

Say: When I hold my hand with the palm up and open, that's your signal to make soft, slow, sad music. When I close my hand into a fist, that's your signal to stop making music.

Let children make music for a couple of minutes, then close your fist to stop the music. Say: It was a sad day when Jesus died, but there's much more to the story.

Ask:

• What happened on the third day after Jesus died?

Say: Jesus rose from the dead and lives with God in heaven.

Ask:

• How does it make you feel to know that Jesus is alive today?

Say: Now let's make happy music with our instruments to celebrate Jesus' resurrection.

Ask:

• What do you think happy music might sound like?

Hold your palm open to have the children make happy music for a couple of minutes, then close your fist to stop the music.

Say: That was wonderful music! I'm so happy that Jesus is alive

today. Let's thank God for that right now.

Pray: Jesus, thank you for dying for us. We're happy to know that you are alive in heaven with God today. We praise you, Jesus. Amen.

MARK 15:33–16:20

THEME:
Jesus is alive!

SUMMARY:
Use this creative storytelling idea to teach children about Jesus' death, resurrection, and ascension.

PREPARATION:
You'll need a Bible.

Have children sit on the floor in a circle. Open your Bible to Mark 15:33–16:20 and show children the passage. Say: This story in the Bible tells about when Jesus died, was buried, and came back to life. I need you to help me tell the story. Have children do the motions with you as you tell the story.

Jesus died upon the cross. (Rub your eyes as if crying.)

He was buried in a grave. *(Bow your head.)*

For three sad days, our Lord was dead *(count to three)*,

But then came Sunday morning. *(Rest one forearm on top of the other. Raise the top forearm to show the sun rising.)*

When the women came to see *(have children stand up while holding hands)*,

Jesus' body was not there. *(Hang your head in sadness.)*

He'd risen from the dead! *(Jump up and cheer.)*

He talked and walked with all his friends. *(Walk around and shake hands.)*

He said, "Go tell the world. *(Move your hands as if they were mouths.)*

If the people will believe in me *(spread your hands to indicate all the people)*,

They'll be my forever friends." *(Hug yourself.)*

Then Jesus went up, up, up into heaven *(stand on tiptoes and then jump)*,

And we have a job to do. *(Have each child tell the child next to him or her that Jesus is alive.)*

MARK 16:1-6, 19

THEME:
Jesus is risen.

SUMMARY:
Use this song to teach children that Jesus died for our sins and rose from the dead because he loves us.

PREPARATION:
You'll need a Bible.

Have children sit in a circle. Say: **Because Jesus loves us, he died on the cross for our sins. That means he died for all the things we do wrong so we can live with Jesus in heaven.**

Open your Bible to Mark 16:1-6, 19, and show children the passage. Say: **This passage tells about the women going to Jesus' tomb after he died on the cross and was buried. But Jesus wasn't in the tomb because he had risen from the dead.**

Read aloud Mark 16:1-6, 19. Ask:

• **How do you think the women felt when they discovered that Jesus was risen? Why?**

• **How do you feel knowing that Jesus died and rose again** for you and me? Why?

Lead children in this song sung to the tune of "Are You Sleeping?"

> **Christ is risen. Christ is risen.**
> **Yes, he is. Yes, he is.**
> **Risen for creation,**
> **And for every nation.**
> **Yes, he is. Yes, he is.**
>
> **Christ went to heaven.**
> **Christ went to heaven.**
> **Yes, he did. Yes, he did.**
> **It was so amazing;**
> **People stood there gazing.**
> **Yes, they did. Yes, they did.**

MARK 16:2-4

THEME:

Jesus has risen.

SUMMARY:

Use this craft idea to teach children that the women discovered the stone had been rolled away from Jesus tomb.

PREPARATION:

You'll need a Bible, old newspapers, plastic cups, tempera paint, water, a 9x13 cake pan, a golf ball, a marker, construction paper, and paint shirts.

Before the activity, cover a table with old newspapers. Pour tempera paint into cups and fill one cup with water. Set out the remaining items.

Open your Bible to Mark 16:2-4, and show children the passage. Say: **This passage tells about Jesus' resurrection. After Jesus died and was buried, the women went to Jesus' tomb to anoint his body with oils. But when they got there, they discovered that the stone had been rolled away and Jesus was alive. We're going to make special rolling-stone paintings to help us remember that Jesus has risen from the dead.**

Hold up a golf ball. Say: **This golf ball will be our "stone." We'll take turns dipping the golf ball in the paint and rolling it around to make pretty designs on paper. You'll each get to dip and roll the golf-ball stone five times. While you're waiting for a turn, you can say a fun cheer. It goes like this: One roll, two rolls, three, four, five. We know Jesus is alive!**

Lead children in saying the cheer, then place a sheet of paper inside the cake pan. Show children how to dip the golf ball into a cup of paint, then place the golf ball in the cake pan and gently tip the cake pan from side to side. Point out the interesting designs the ball makes as it rolls over the paper. Rinse off the ball in the cup of water, dip it in a second color of paint, and roll the ball over the paper again. Repeat the process three more times. Remove the painting to dry. Place a new sheet of paper in the cake pan.

Let each child make a painting by dipping and rolling the ball five times. Make sure you rinse off the ball between colors. Lead children in saying the cheer as each child creates his or her painting. Help the children use the marker to write their names on their paintings. Set the completed paintings aside to dry.

Used with permission from *First and Favorite Bible Lessons for Preschoolers* © 1996 Beth Rowland Wolf and Bonnie Temple. Published by Group Publishing, Inc., P.O. Box 481, Loveland, CO 80539.
www.grouppublishing.com

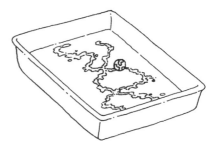

LUKE

"Today in the town of David a Savior has been born to you; he is Christ the Lord."

Luke 2:11

LUKE
1:26-33

THEME:
Jesus loves me.

SUMMARY:
Use this affirmation idea to teach children that they are special to Jesus.

PREPARATION:
You'll need a Bible.

Have the kids scatter around the middle of the room. Open your Bible to Luke 1:26-33, and show children the passage. Say: **In this Bible story, the angel told Mary what the name of her special son would be. It was Jesus.**

Show the kids how to stomp out each syllable of Jesus' name. Say: **Your name was chosen especially for you, too. Let's take turns saying our first names out loud. We'll all stomp with our feet one time for each part of each person's name.**

Have children stomp once for each syllable of each person's first name. After they have mastered this, have children stomp out the phrase "Jesus loves [name]!" inserting each child's name. Ask:

• How does it feel to know that Jesus loves you?

• How can we show Jesus we love him?

Close by having children stomp out the phrase, "We love Jesus!"

LUKE
1:37

THEME:
God can do anything.

SUMMARY:
Use this object lesson to teach children that nothing is impossible with God.

PREPARATION:
You'll need a Bible and supplies as described below.

Before children arrive, set up several stations where children can try difficult tasks. You might set out new jars of food (such as jelly or baby food) for them to open, pails of rocks or sand for them to lift, a box for them to fill with blocks and lift, or sacks of potatoes and jugs of water for them to carry. Make sure that at least one station is impossible for them to do.

Gather children together and say: **I have a muscle challenge for you today. Take a few minutes and try the jobs at these stations. We'll see how strong and powerful you are.** Explain what children are to do at each station, then let children choose which stations they'd like to try. After a few minutes, gather children and ask:

• **Were any of these jobs too hard for you to do?**

• **What was it like to try such hard jobs?**

• **Do you think God could do all these jobs? Why or why not?**

Open your Bible to Luke 1:37, show children the passage, and read it aloud. Say: **This verse tells us that God is all-powerful. Nothing is too hard for God. There is no one who is as powerful as our God.**

Ask:

• **How does it feel to know that our God is super powerful?**

Say: **It's good to know that God is so powerful that nothing is too hard for him. God is strong enough to take care of us, no matter what hard things we have to do!**

LUKE 2:1-7

THEME:

Jesus is the greatest gift of all.

SUMMARY:

Use this party to teach children about the birth of Jesus.

PREPARATION:

You'll need a Bible, party decorations, a wrapped package, cupcakes, punch, party supplies as described below, paper sacks, craft supplies, and candy.

Before the party, roll sheets of construction paper to form cone-shaped hats. Glue the edges. Punch two holes across from each other on the bottom edge of each hat and attach ribbons for the tie. You'll need one hat for each child.

Gather children together and show them a package wrapped in birthday gift wrap. Ask:

• **What did you do to celebrate your last birthday?** Allow time for the children to share their party memories.

Ask:

• **Whose birthday do we celebrate on Christmas?**

Say: **We're going to have a**

birthday party for Jesus today. Let's decorate our room for his party. Give children crepe paper streamers with tape attached to the ends. Have children decorate the table or room for a party. Hang balloons over your table. As you decorate, talk about ways we make birthdays special.

Have children sit in a circle. Open your Bible to Luke 2:1-7, and show children the passage. Say: **This story tells us about when Jesus was born. I need you to help me tell the story by following my actions.** Have children follow your actions as you say the following rhyme:

Clap your hands. *(Clap hands.)*

Give a shout. *(Shout "hooray!" and throw your hands in the air.)*

We know what Christmas is all about! *(Point to yourself and nod.)*

Long ago *(make an arc with your right hand)*,

Far away *(make an arc with your left hand)*,

A baby boy was born this special day. *(Rock arms.)*

Mary wrapped him *(pretend to wrap a blanket around a baby)*,

Laid him down *(reach down, palms up)*,

In a manger in Bethlehem town. *(Make the peak of the stable with your hands.)*

Baby Jesus *(rock arms)*,

Fast asleep *(lay cheek on folded hands)*

In a room with cows and sheep! *(Make animal noises.)*

Angels sang. *(Cup hands around your mouth.)*

Shepherds heard. *(Cup hands around your ears.)*

They hurried to the stable. *(Run in place.)*

They spread the word! *(Cup hands around your mouth.)*

Happy Birthday, Jesus! Happy Christmas Day! *(Have children repeat phrase and raise arms in the air.)*

Say: **We give presents to people who have birthdays. But on Jesus' birthday, we celebrate by giving gifts to people.**

Ask:

• **Why do we give gifts to each other?**

• **What gifts could we give to Jesus that would make him happy?**

Say: **On Jesus' birthday, we're the ones who get the best gift of all—Jesus!**

Give children the plain, cone-shaped party hats. Have them decorate the hats with foil stars and other Christmas stickers and seals. Help children tie on their hats to wear as they eat their snack. Hand out party blowers.

Have children sing "Happy Birthday, Jesus" as you bring out the cupcakes. Before children have the cake and punch, lead them in the following prayer using their party blowers.

Thank you, God, for the birth of your Son. *(Blow horns.)*

Thank you, Jesus, that you are the one. *(Blow horns.)*

You are the greatest gift, it's true. *(Blow horns.)*

We love you, Jesus, yes we do! *(Blow horns.)*

After children have finished their snack, provide paper lunch bags, scissors, glue, and assorted fabric and paper scraps. Have children each cut and glue scraps to the outside of the bag to make a manger scene. Use cotton balls for sheep, paper doilies for angel wings, and glitter or foil for stars. When children are finished, help them each fold over an inch at the top of the bag and punch two holes. Fill the bag with a candy cane and a few other treats. Thread ribbon through the holes and tie a bow. Have children take their goodie bags, hats, and party blowers home as a reminder of Jesus' birthday.

LUKE 2:1-20

THEME:
God sent his Son.

SUMMARY:
Use this object lesson to teach children that Jesus is the real meaning of Christmas.

PREPARATION:
You'll need a Bible and a sack filled with small, unbreakable Christmas decorations. Include Santa ornaments, elves, wreaths, stars, nativity scenes, Rudolph, shepherds, wise men, stables, and presents. Have mangers and several figures of baby Jesus, Mary, and Joseph.

Gather children together and have them take turns removing decorations from the sack. Then have them put the decorations in two separate piles. One pile represents the real meaning of Christmas, and the other pile represents things that aren't the real meaning of Christmas.

Say: **Let's put away the Santas, reindeer, elves, and all those things that are fun but aren't really what Christmas is all about.**

Open your Bible to Luke 2:1-20,

and show children the passage. Tell them a paraphrase of the story.

Say: **Now I'd like you to tell me the real story of Christmas using these decorations.**

Let children each a have a turn telling the Christmas story with the ornaments. Then close in prayer, thanking God for sending the greatest gift of all—his Son, Jesus.

LUKE 2:10

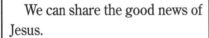

THEME:

We can share the good news of Jesus.

SUMMARY:

Use this craft idea to teach children about the angel telling the shepherds the good news of Jesus' birth.

PREPARATION:

You'll need a Bible, blue and white construction paper, scissors, cotton swabs, pencils, glue, a pie pan, large white paper doilies, facial tissues, and narrow white ribbon.

Before class, cut sheets of blue and white construction paper so you have two 6x9-inch pieces for each child. Then fold the pieces in half to make 6x4½-inch cards. Cut narrow white ribbon into six-inch lengths, providing one piece for each child.

Arrange for adult helpers to assist children with this craft.

Give each child one precut sheet of both blue and white construction paper and a pencil. Help each preschooler lay one hand on the white paper with the thumb laying along the fold. Then have adult helpers assist children in tracing their hands. Have adults cut out the hand tracings, taking care not to cut the fold of the papers.

Invite children to open the hand shapes to form "wings." Set out glue in a pie pan and give each child a cotton swab. Help preschoolers glue the wings inside the folded blue cards so the tips of the fingers touch the tops of the blue cards.

Give each child a large paper doily, two facial tissues, and a piece of narrow white ribbon. Show children how to wad the facial tissues into a ball, press the ball into the center of the doily, and pinch the doily together under the ball to form a head. Have adult helpers tie a white ribbon around the "neck" of each doily. Help each child put two lines of glue near the center of the wings and press the doily against the glue. The bottom of the angel should be even with the bottom of the card. When the glue dries, the angel will stand on its own. Allow fifteen minutes of drying time.

As the angels dry, have children sit in a circle. Open your Bible to Luke 2:10, show children the passage, and read it aloud. Say: **When Jesus was born, an angel appeared to the shepherds and told them that the Christ child was born in Bethlehem.**

Ask:

• **How do you think the shepherds felt when they saw the angel?**

• **How can we tell others the good news about Jesus?**

Teach children the following rhyme:

Angels white, angels bright,
Angels in the sky tonight.
"Go to Bethlehem," they say.
"See the baby in the hay."

After the angels have dried, let children wave their angels as they say the rhyme to each other.

LUKE 2:11

THEME:

Jesus came to let us be a part of God's family.

SUMMARY:

Use this fun puzzle to help your children understand that Jesus came to let us be a part of God's family because everyone is important in God's family.

PREPARATION:

You'll need a Bible, a copy of the "God Is With Us" handout (p. 57), glue, stiff paper, gold spray paint, scissors, a cookie sheet, rigatoni noodles, a hole punch, watercolor markers, and one eighteen-inch length of yarn for each child.

Before the activity, paint the back of the stiff paper with gold paint. When the paint is dry, glue the "God Is With Us" handout to the front of the paper. Cut the puzzle apart then reassemble it on a cookie sheet with the picture facing up.

Show children the puzzle you've prepared. Ask:

• **What do you see in this picture?**

Encourage children to point out Mary, Joseph, Jesus, the shepherds, and the other details in the puzzle picture. Open your Bible to Luke 2:11, show children the passage, and read it aloud.

Say: **God is with us. God sent his Son, Jesus, to earth for us. When we believe in Jesus, we are all a part of God's family, just as these puzzle pieces are a part of one puzzle.**

Pull out one of the puzzle pieces, being careful not to let the children see the painted back. Say: **If there's a piece missing, the puzzle isn't finished, is it? So just as all of the pieces are important to the puzzle, we're all important in God's family. We're each very special.**

Turn over one of the pieces, and show children the shiny back. Punch a hole in the piece, then thread a piece of yarn through the hole. Tie a knot in the yarn to create a necklace. Slip the necklace over your head. Show the children the shiny side of the puzzle piece, and say: **I'm special because I'm me, all by myself.** Then turn the puzzle piece over to the picture side, and say: **But I'm also a special part of God's family. You're special too.**

Give children each a turn to tell something about themselves that is special. Then let each child choose a piece of the puzzle and one of the pieces of yarn. Be sure that you have enough puzzle pieces for all your children. Punch holes in the puzzle pieces, and help children thread the yarn through the holes. Set out rigatoni noodles, and let children add noodles to their necklaces. You may want to let children color the noodles with watercolor markers.

As children work, remind them that God is with us. When children have finished their necklaces, tie knots in the yarn, and help children hang the necklaces around their necks to remind them that they are a special part of God's family.

Used with permission from *First and Favorite Bible Lessons for Preschoolers* © 1996 Beth Rowland Wolf and Bonnie Temple. Published by Group Publishing, Inc., P.O. Box 481, Loveland, CO 80539. www.grouppublishing.com

LUKE 2:41-52

THEME:
Jesus grows wise.

SUMMARY:
Use this creative storytelling activity to teach children about Jesus as a twelve-year-old boy.

PREPARATION:
You'll need a Bible.

GOD IS WITH US

O pen your Bible to Luke 2:41-52, and show children the passage. Say: **This Bible story is about Jesus when he was a twelve-year-old boy. Let's act out the story together.** Have preschoolers repeat your words and actions to this fun drama.

I'm Mary, Jesus' mom. *(Pretend to cradle a baby in your arms.)*

I'm Joseph, Jesus' dad. *(Stand with your hands on your hips.)*

We're taking Jesus to Jerusalem for the Passover Feast. *(Walk in place.)*

It's time to get some sleep! *(Lay your head on your hands.)*

We must keep traveling to Jerusalem. *(Walk in place.)*

In Jerusalem, we celebrate the Passover. *(Clap your hands.)*

It's time to go back home. *(Pretend to pack things up.)*

Where is Jesus? *(Put your hands over your eyebrows, as if searching.)*

We must find him. *(Walk in place.)*

We looked for Jesus for three days. *(Hold up three fingers.)*

Jesus is in God's house, talking to the teachers. *(Make praying hands, then cup your hands around your mouth.)*

We told him we were worried! *(Put your hands on your cheeks and shake your head back and forth.)*

Jesus explains he wanted to talk about God. *(Stretch your hands outward.)*

It's time for Jesus to go back home with us. *(Walk in place.)*

Jesus obeyed his parents, and he grew up to be wise. *(Squat, then stand up slowly with your finger to your temple.)*

LUKE 3:11

THEME:
Share with your neighbors.

SUMMARY:
Use this devotion idea to teach children that it pleases Jesus when we share what we have with others.

PREPARATION:
You'll need a Bible and copies of the steppingstone handout (p. 60).

Before the activity, cut out a "Steppingstone to Sharing" handout for each person.

G ather children together, and teach them the words and motions of this song to the tune of "Twinkle, Twinkle, Little Star."

> How I, how I love to share *(walk to the middle of the circle),*
>
> With my neighbors every-where. *(Walk out.)*
>
> It pleases Jesus when I do. *(Point up.)*
>
> It makes us happy, me and you. *(Shake hands with someone, then join hands in a circle again.)*
>
> How I, how I love to share *(walk to the middle of the circle),*
>
> With my neighbors every-where. *(Walk out.)*

Have children sit in a circle. Open your Bible to Luke 3:11, show children the passage, and read the verse aloud. Ask:

• **Why do you think it pleases Jesus when we share with others?**

• **How do you feel when you share with someone? Why?**

• **How do you think others feel when you share with them? Why?**

Give each child a steppingstone handout. Read the words on the handout to the children. Say: **Let's do a special prayer activity to ask God to help us remember to share what we have with others. We'll each have a turn to pray for something specific to share, like food, clothing, or kindness.**

Pray: **Dear God, thank you for your gifts.** Place your steppingstone on the floor in front of you, and step on it. **Help me to share** [say

something specific like food that you can share] **with others.** Have the child to your right step on his or her steppingstone and say, "Help me to share [something specific] with others." You may need to prompt children. Continue around the circle until each child has had a turn to pray. Close with everyone saying: **Amen.**

Let children take their stepping-stones home as a reminder to share with others.

LUKE 4:8b

THEME:

We're created to worship God.

SUMMARY:

Use this devotion idea to teach children that God wants us to love and serve only him.

PREPARATION:

You'll need a Bible and bags of Hershey's Hugs.

Have children sit in a circle. Say: **Hugs show a special kind of love. There are all kinds of hugs. There are bear hugs that are tight and powerful; there are group hugs which get very crowded;**

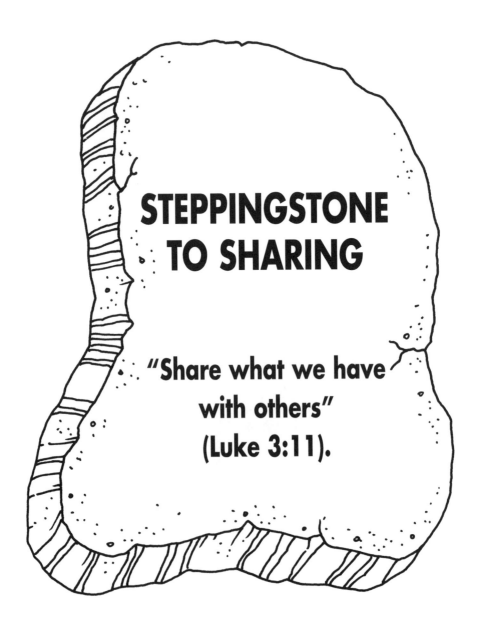

STEPPINGSTONE TO SHARING

"Share what we have with others" (Luke 3:11).

there are hugs that hang on very long; and there are hugs that are short and sweet.

Ask:

• **Who gives you hugs?**

• **What kind of hugs do you give others?**

Say: **Hugs are important because they show love and care. I want to give each of you a special hug.**

Give each child a Hershey's Hugs candy and let them eat it. Ask:

• **How did this hug make you feel? Why?**

Say: **Giving you those hugs made me feel great! That's the special thing about hugs.**

Ask:

• **How can we share hugs with God?**

• **What can we do to show God we love him?**

Open your Bible to Luke 4:8b, show children the passage, and read it aloud. Say: **This tells us that God wants us to show him a special kind of love. He wants us to worship and serve only him.**

Ask:

• **How can we worship and serve God?**

Say: **Let's worship God together in prayer. I will start praying, and each time I pause, you say, "We worship you."**

Lead children in the following prayer:

Dear God, thank you for hugs. *(Pause and have children say, "We worship you.")*

Thank you for those who give us hugs. *(Pause and have children say, "We worship you.")*

Hear our songs and shouts of love. *(Pause and have children say, "We worship you.")*

Thank you for your love for us. *(Pause and have children say, "We worship you.")*

In Jesus' name we pray. Amen.

LUKE 6:38

THEME:

God loves a cheerful giver.

SUMMARY:

Use this service idea to teach children that God wants us to give generously to others.

PREPARATION:

You'll need a Bible, heavy butcher paper or pieces of poster board taped together to make a piece large enough to trace an adult body on it, double-sided tape, a marker, and several coins.

Before the activity, find out

about a need that the children could make a donation to help. This might be related to a needy family, an organization that helps people in need, or a missionary your church supports. Send a note to parents, explaining your project and telling them how you'll use the children's donations.

Trace the outline of an adult on the paper.

Have children stand in a circle with their hands out in front of them and their palms touching. Have one child stand in the middle of the circle. Show the children a coin, and say: **I'm going to pretend to put this coin in each of your hands. I'll really only give it to one of you, but all of you need to pretend you get the coin. When I'm finished,** [name of the person in the middle of the circle] **will guess who has the coin. Keep your hands closed tightly so** [name of the person in the middle of the circle] **can't tell where the coin is!**

Move around to each child in the circle, pretending to drop the coin into each child's hands. Drop the coin into one child's hands. Finish moving around the circle. Turn to the child in the middle of the circle and ask:

• **Who do you think has the coin?**

Let the child guess. Then let the child who has the coin move to the middle and the child in the middle return to the circle. Play again. Continue the game giving each child a turn in the middle.

Open your Bible to Luke 6:38, show children the passage, and read it aloud. Say: **This tells us that God wants us to give generously to other people, and if you give to other people, God will give to you. In our game, we had a coin to play with. But we're going to do a project that will give others a chance to have coins to keep. Instead of one coin, we'll have many coins. We're going to give our coins to** [name of family, organization, or missionary you've chosen].

Explain the project you've chosen to save coins for. If possible, show a sample of the project or illustrate the results.

Have the children gather around the butcher paper or poster board outline you traced ahead of time. Say: **This shape represents** [name of project] **that we're saving our money for. We can all help by giving what we have. Every time you come to class, bring whatever coins you can. We're going to stick them inside this shape until the shape is all filled up**.

Show the children how to tape some of the coins you brought inside the shape. Start along the inside edge of the outline and place the coins next to each other so they're touching.

Say: **When you bring your coins to class, you can tape them inside our shape. God loves a cheerful giver. And he promises that when we give, he will give back to us.**

Ask:

• **Why does God want us to be cheerful when we give?**

• **Why does God want to give good things to us?**

As children bring in pennies or other coins, help them tape the coins to the inside of the outline you've drawn. When the outline is completely filled with coins, have children present the offering to the church or organization. Praise the children for their generous giving, and remind them that God loves a cheerful giver.

LUKE 8:5-8

THEME:

God's love grows in our hearts.

SUMMARY:

Use this object lesson to teach children about the parable of the sower.

PREPARATION:

You'll need a Bible and a large zipper-sealed bag of soil.

Have children sit in a circle. Open your Bible to Luke 8:5-8, and hold up the passage for preschoolers to see. Say: **In this story, Jesus tells about a man who planted some seeds to grow some plants.**

Ask:

• **What do you think the man needs to make his seeds grow?**

Say: **He needs sunshine and water, and he also needs the good dirt God made. But when the man planted his seeds, some fell into the road.**

Ask:

• **What do you think happened to the seeds that fell in the road?**

Say: **Some birds ate the seeds in the road. Some seeds fell on rocks and some under sticker bushes.**

Ask:

• **Do you think the plants could grow in the rocks or under the sticker bushes? Why not?**

Say: **The plants didn't grow in the rocks because they were too hard for the seeds. They didn't grow under the sticker bushes because the seeds were choked and they died. But some seeds fell in good soil, which is another name for dirt.**

Pass around the bag of soil for

children to reach in and feel the dirt. You may want to have wet wipes for the children to clean their hands when they're done. Read aloud Luke 8:8a. Say: **That means the seeds that fell in the good soil grew lots and lots of plants. Good soil helps plants to grow. When we love God, our hearts are like the good soil because God's love grows in us.**

Let's thank God for making our hearts like good soil.

Pray: **Dear God, thank you so much for making our hearts like good soil. Help your love grow in us. In Jesus' name, amen.**

LUKE 8:22-25

THEME:

We can trust Jesus to help us.

SUMMARY:

Use this storytelling idea to teach children that Jesus calmed a storm and saved the disciples.

PREPARATION:

You'll need a Bible.

Open your Bible to Luke 8:22-25, and show children the passage. Say: **This story tells about Jesus calming a storm. I need you to help me tell the story by acting out the motions with me.**

Lead children in the following action story:

One day Jesus said to his disciples, "Let's go to the other side of the lake." *(Wave your arm to tell everyone to come along.)*

So they all got in the boat *(climb into a boat, hamming it up as though the boat might tip)*

And they rowed out to sea. *(Make rowing motions.)*

Jesus fell asleep *(lay your head on your hands)*

And a big, fierce wind blew against the boat. *(Wave arms like big gusts of wind, and make a "wooooo" sound.)*

The water washed up over the boat. They were all in great danger. *(Sway back and forth and pretend to be frightened.)*

"Jesus!" they yelled. "We're going to drown!" *(Pretend to shake Jesus and yell, "Jesus! Jesus!")*

Jesus awoke and he calmed the storm *(hold out your hand against the wind)*

And the wind died down. *(Let your arms wave violently like the wind and then die down.)*

The disciples were amazed. "Who is this?" they cried. *(Look amazed and raise arms as if asking a question.)*

"**Even the wind and the waves obey him.**" *(Nod head "yes.")*

Ask:

• **How would you have felt if you were one of the disciples in the boat?**

• **Can you think of a time you needed Jesus' help?**

• **How did Jesus help you?**

Close by praying: **Jesus, thank you for calming the storm for the disciples. Please calm the stormy times in our lives. Amen.**

LUKE 10:25-37

THEME:

God wants us to help our neighbors.

SUMMARY:

Use this service idea to teach children that God is pleased when we help others and love our neighbors.

PREPARATION:

You'll need a Bible, zipper sandwich bags, cotton balls, plastic bandages, and stickers.

Before the activity, make a sample first-aid kit by placing three or four plastic bandages, a few cotton balls, and several stickers in a sandwich bag. Decorate the outside of the bag with a few stickers.

Open your Bible to Luke 10:25-37, and show the passage to the children. Say: **This is a story that Jesus told about being a good neighbor. One day a man was traveling to another town, and some robbers attacked him. They tore his clothes, took his money, and beat him up. Then they left him by the side of the road to die. Two men walked by and didn't even help him. Then a man from Samaria stopped to help. People from Samaria were enemies of this man, but the Samaritan was the only one to stop. He bandaged the hurt man's cuts and scrapes.**

Ask:

• **How do you think the hurt man felt when the first two men didn't even stop to help him? Why?**

• **Who was the good neighbor in our story?**

• **Did you ever help someone? Tell us about it.**

Say: **The man in our story needed someone to bandage up his cuts and scrapes. Tell us about a time you needed a bandage.**

Give children time to respond.

Then say: **It's good to have bandages on hand in case someone gets a scrape or cut. Let's use bandages and some other things to make first-aid kits so we'll be ready to help someone who's hurt. Then we can be a good neighbor to someone in need.**

Hold up the sample first-aid kit you assembled before class. Say: **We can use cotton balls to clean the dirt off a cut before we put a bandage on it. We can use stickers to cheer up a friend who's hurt or sick. You can give your friend the sticker and say, "I love you." I put a few stickers on my bag to make it pretty.**

Distribute bags, and help children assemble their first-aid kits. Let them choose three or four bandages, a few cotton balls, and several stickers. Set out enough stickers so that children can decorate their bags, too. As they work, remind them that God is pleased when we help others, and he wants us to love our neighbors.

Used with permission from *First and Favorite Bible Lessons for Preschoolers* © 1996 Beth Rowland Wolf and Bonnie Temple. Published by Group Publishing, Inc., P.O. Box 481, Loveland, CO 80539.
www.grouppublishing.com

LUKE 10:38-42

THEME:

Jesus wants us to spend time with him.

SUMMARY:

Use this chant to teach children about Jesus visiting Mary and Martha.

PREPARATION:

You'll need a Bible.

Open your Bible to Luke 10:38-42, and show children the passage. Say: **This story tells about Jesus visiting Mary and Martha. Mary wanted to spend time with Jesus and hear his words. Martha wanted to serve Jesus by making him comfortable and giving him a good meal. Martha was angry that Mary wasn't helping her. But Jesus said that Mary made the right choice because she chose to spend time with him. Let's learn a song about the story.**

Begin by asking children to clap their hands together and then slap their knees, clap their hands together and slap their knees, and so on, until they have picked up on the beat. Then sing the following chant with the same rhythm as the childhood rhyme, "Who Stole the Cookies From the Cookie Jar?"

Who sat with Jesus when he came to visit?

Mary sat with Jesus when he came to visit!

Who, Mary? Yes, Mary!

I agree! It's true!

Who was too busy to hear Jesus talk?

Martha was too busy to hear Jesus talk!

Who, Martha? Yes, Martha!

I agree! It's true!

Who knows that we must listen when Jesus talks?

I know that we must listen when Jesus talks!

Who, me? Yes, you!

I agree! It's true!

Say: **Let's all try to be like Mary and take time to listen to Jesus.**

LUKE 11:1-4

THEME:

Jesus teaches us to pray.

SUMMARY:

Use this prayer to teach children how to pray.

PREPARATION:

You'll need a Bible.

O pen your Bible to Luke 11:1-4, and show children the passage. Say: **This passage is known as the Lord's Prayer. The disciples asked Jesus for help in learning to pray, so he taught his friends how to pray using this special prayer. We're going to learn a version of this prayer to help us learn to pray.**

Lead children in the words and motions of this prayer:

Jesus taught his friends to pray (place your palms together, like praying hands)

About these five things every day (hold one hand up with fingers spread apart):

God, you are holy, number one. (Touch your thumb.)

Your kingdom come, your will be done. (Touch your index finger.)

Give us all our daily needs. (Touch your middle finger.)

That is subject number three.

Four, forgive us all our sins. (Touch your ring finger.)

Five, all glory belongs to you. (Touch your pinkie.)

I am learning how to pray

(point to yourself)

About these five things every day. *(Run your index finger along the five fingers.)*

LUKE 12:48b

THEME:

God gives us different talents and gifts.

SUMMARY:

Use this affirmation idea to teach children that God wants us to use the gifts he gives us to help others.

PREPARATION:

You'll need a Bible.

Have children stand in a circle. Say: **God is so good to give us different talents and gifts. Let's sing a song, and when we sing about something you're good at, step to the center of the circle. Then you can show us your talent.**

Lead children in singing "I Am Special" to the tune of "Are You Sleeping?" When you reach the bracketed words, have children who are good at that activity step to the center of the circle. After the song, have those children standing in the center of the circle demonstrate their talents. Encourage the rest of the children to clap after each demonstration.

> **I am special; I am special.**
> **If you look, you will see**
> **Someone good at** [hopping],
> **Someone good at** [hopping].
> **Yes, it's me. Yes, it's me.**

After children have shared their hopping talents, repeat the song using whistling, singing, and smiling.

After you've finished singing, say: **It's great that God gives us so many gifts and talents.** Open your Bible to Luke 12:48b, show children the passage, and read it aloud. Say: **This passage means that God expects us to use the gifts that he has given us.**

Ask:

• **Why do you think God gives us many things?**

• **Why does God want us to use the gifts he gives us?**

• **How can we use our gifts to help others?**

Say: **It makes God happy when we use the gifts he has given us to help others. Let's use our gift of smiling today to help brighten someone's day.**

LUKE 15:1-7

THEME:

God cares for us.

SUMMARY:

Use this creative storytelling activity to teach children that God cares for them just as the watchful shepherd cares for his sheep.

PREPARATION:

You'll need a Bible and a photocopy of the "Sheep" handout (p. 71). Before the children arrive, hide the sheep picture in the room.

Open your Bible to Luke 15:1-7, and show the passage to the children. Say: **This is a story that Jesus told about a shepherd and his sheep.**

Ask:

• **What sound does a sheep make?**

• **Who takes care of sheep?**

Say: **Shepherds take good care of their sheep. They lead the sheep to cool water and soft, green grass. They make sure wolves and lions and bears stay away. Let's pretend that I'm the shepherd in Jesus' story and all** of you are the sheep.

Have children get down on their hands and knees and scatter around the room.

Say: **One day a shepherd took his sheep to a beautiful hillside where they could eat green grass and drink water from a cool stream. When evening came, the shepherd gathered all his sheep and counted them one by one.**

Walk around the room and "herd" the children. Have them crawl to the middle of the room and sit down. Count each child as he or she joins the group.

Say: **The shepherd counted one, two, three, four, five, six, seven, eight, nine, ten. He kept counting all the way up to ninety-seven, ninety-eight, ninety-nine. And that was the last sheep he could find. There were supposed to be one hundred sheep. One sheep was missing!**

Ask:

• **What do you think the shepherd did when he found that one of his sheep was gone?**

Say: **The shepherd was so worried that he left all the other sheep and went to look for the sheep that was lost. Do you know what? There's a lost sheep somewhere in our classroom. Why don't you help me find it?**

Have children help you hunt for

the sheep picture. When someone finds it, have the children cheer.

Say: **The shepherd was so happy when he found the little lost sheep! He picked it up and cuddled it and carried it over his shoulders. Then he called out to his friends and neighbors, "Look! My sheep was lost, but now I've found it! Come celebrate with me!" That's how God feels about you. He loves you and promises to take care of you and protect you all the time.**

LUKE 15:8-10

THEME:
You are Jesus' treasure.

SUMMARY:
Use this object lesson to teach children the parable of the lost coin.

PREPARATION:
You'll need a Bible and five large play coins for each child. These need to be larger than a fifty-cent piece.

Before the activity, hide five coins in the room for each child.

After children arrive, have them each find five coins. Then have them sit in a circle, set their coins on the floor in front of them, and close their eyes. Take one coin away from each child. Have children open their eyes. After children realize their coins are missing, ask:

• **How did you feel when you saw that your coin was gone?**

Open your Bible to Luke 15:8-10, show children the passage, and read it aloud. Then ask:

• **How do you think this woman felt when she lost her coin?**

• **Why was she so happy when she found her coin?**

Give children's coins back to them to keep. Say: **Jesus is sad when one of us chooses not to stay with him and follow him. Jesus searches and searches for anyone who isn't following him. And Jesus brings that person back to follow him. You are Jesus' treasure.**

SHEEP

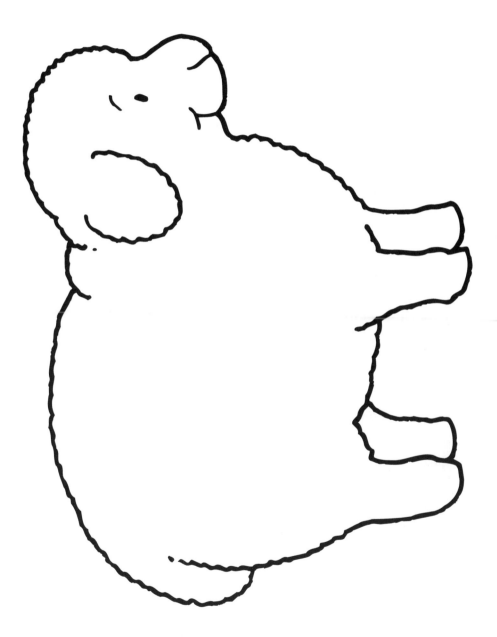

LUKE 19:1-10

THEME:

Jesus loves everyone

SUMMARY:

Use this devotion to teach children that Jesus loves us just as he loved Zacchaeus.

PREPARATION:

You'll need a Bible, brown poster board, a black marker, masking tape, and green balloons.

Before class, cut out a 3-foot-tall tree trunk from brown poster board. Use a marker to draw vertical lines of bark. Tape the trunk to the wall. Then tape inflated green balloons to the top of the tree for leaves. Sit at the foot of the sycamore tree during the lesson.

Have children sit in a circle. Show children Luke 19:1-10 in your Bible, and tell them a paraphrase of the story. Say: **Jesus loved Zacchaeus very much, and Jesus wanted Zacchaeus to love him.**

Ask:

• **How did Zacchaeus show Jesus that he loved him?**

• **How can you show Jesus that you love him?**

Establish a rhythm by having children slap their thighs twice, clap once, slap thighs twice, clap once. Once the rhythm is comfortable, introduce this chant:

Je-sus loved Za-cchae-us, Je-sus loves [child's name].

Repeat the chant inserting each child's name. Then close in prayer thanking Jesus for loving us.

LUKE 24:1-12

THEME:

Jesus is alive!

SUMMARY:

Use this party to remind children of the surprise the women must have felt when they saw that Jesus was alive.

PREPARATION:

You'll need a Bible, rocks, party invitations, gray construction paper, scissors, refrigerator box, piece of white cloth, three crosses made from poster board, biblical costumes, refrigerated biscuit dough, marshmallows, butter, cinnamon, sugar, baking pans, an empty piñata, plastic bat, and wrapped candies.

Hand out to children real rocks with the party invitations wrapped around them with rubber bands. Using gray construction paper, cut out a stone path that leads to the party area. For decorations, make a "tomb" out of a refrigerator box. Inside the tomb, lay a shroud (a piece of white cloth). Tape three poster board crosses to a wall. Have volunteers dress in biblical costumes similar to the days of the first Easter.

Make Resurrection Buns for a snack. For each bun, wrap unbaked refrigerated biscuit dough around a marshmallow and tightly close the edges. Roll the dough ball in melted butter and then in cinnamon and sugar. Bake the buns at 375 degrees until lightly browned.

Have children follow the stone path into the party area and sit in a circle. Say: **Welcome to our "Jesus is alive!" party.** Open your Bible to Luke 24:1-12 and show children the passage. **This passage tells us how Jesus' women friends went to the tomb where he was buried to bring spices for his body. But as the women got close to the tomb, the giant stone that sealed the tomb shut had been rolled away, and Jesus' body was gone. Jesus was alive! Today we'll celebrate that Jesus rose from the dead.**

Play the game Rock 'n' Roll Relay. Form teams of four and have each team line up at one end of the room. On your signal, have the first child in line lie down and roll on the ground to the opposite wall, get up, and run back to his or her team. (It won't be easy for children to run back because they'll be dizzy.) Continue until each team member has rolled to the wall and run back to his or her team. After the relay, remind children that the heavy stone was rolled away from Jesus' tomb and that Jesus died and rose again!

Next hang an empty piñata from the ceiling. Have kids take turns swinging at the piñata with a plastic bat. For safety, don't blindfold children and keep them at a safe distance while waiting for their turns. When the piñata pops, nothing will fall out. Have kids sit on the floor. Ask:

• **How did you feel when nothing came out of the piñata?**

• **How do you think the women felt when Jesus wasn't in the tomb where he had been buried?**

Gently toss candy to the children. Ask:

• **How did you feel when you got candy?**

• **How is that like the way the disciples felt when Jesus rose from the dead?**

Say: **Let's thank Jesus for dying for our sins and rising on the third day**.

Serve Resurrection Buns for a snack. When kids bite into the Resurrection Buns, they'll find them empty—just as Jesus' tomb was.

JOHN

"No, the Father himself loves you because you have loved me and have believed that I came from God."

John 16:27

JOHN 1:1-4, 14

THEME:
Jesus is the light of the world.

SUMMARY:
Use this finger play to teach children that Jesus and God are one and the same.

PREPARATION:
You'll need a Bible.

Open your Bible to John 1:1-4, 14, and show children the passage. Read the Scripture aloud. Say: **This passage tells us that even before the world was made, Jesus was with God and is God.**

Jesus loves us so much that he shines his light into our hearts by filling us with his love.

Ask:

• **How do you feel knowing Jesus loves you?**

• **How can you show others Jesus' love?**

Teach children the words and motions to this rhyme:

Jesus is God *(point up)*,

And God is love. *(Hug self.)*

God sent Jesus from above. *(Cross and rock arms as if holding a baby.)*

Jesus is God *(point up)*,

And God is light. *(Flash fingers.)*

The love of Jesus shines so bright. *(Flash fingers at a friend.)*

Jesus is God. *(Point up.)*

God came to us. *(Point to a friend, then to yourself.)*

Thank you, God, for JESUS! *(Fold hands in prayer.)*

Close in prayer, thanking God for his Son Jesus and for his light that shines in our hearts.

JOHN 1:43-51

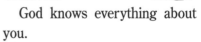

THEME:
God knows everything about you.

SUMMARY:
Use this game to teach children that God loves us so much that he knows all about us.

PREPARATION:
You'll need a Bible, a pen, three plastic foam cups, a marble or other small object, and a tray.

Before the activity, mark a small dot on a cup. Try to make it visible to you and only you. Place the three cups upside down on the tray.

ather children together and say: **Let's start our time together with a game. I have three cups and a marble. I'll place the marble under a cup and you can move the cups around and I'll guess where the marble is.**

Place the marble under the cup with the dot on it. Have a child move the cups about, and guess where the marble is. Let children each have a turn moving the cups so you can guess where the marble is. Make sure the marble goes under the cup with the dot on it every time. After a minute, set the tray out of children's reach. Ask:

• **Why do you think I always knew where the marble was?**

Show children the mark on the cup. Say: **I had a helper. This mark made it easy for me to find the marble.**

Ask:

• **Did you know that just as I always knew where the marble was, God always knows where you are and what you're doing?**

Say: **In fact, God knows everything about you.**

Open your Bible to John 1:43-51, and show the passage to the children. Say: **In this passage, Jesus showed us how well God knows us. Once Jesus amazed a man named Nathanael. Nathanael didn't understand why his friends thought** Jesus was so special, and he didn't even want to meet Jesus. But when Nathanael finally met Jesus, Jesus told Nathanael he had seen what Nathanael was doing, and knew Nathanael before they had even met. Nathanael began to understand why Jesus is so special! **Just as Jesus knew about Nathanael, God knows all about you.**

Ask:

• **How do you feel knowing that God loves you so much that he knows all about you? Why?**

Say: **God has known us, and loved us, from the beginning of time.**

JOHN 2:1-11

THEME:

God can work miracles.

SUMMARY:

Use this craft idea to teach children that miracles are possible with God.

PREPARATION:

You'll need a Bible, buttermilk, one-inch-wide sponge brushes, pastel construction paper, and colored chalk.

Before the activity, cover the

table with a vinyl cloth or have a sponge handy to wipe off the table when you're done with the craft.

Have children each dip their sponge brush into the buttermilk, and smear the buttermilk onto the construction paper, covering the entire page. Then have them draw a picture with the colored chalk directly onto the wet buttermilk surface. The buttermilk will keep the chalk drawing from smearing or smudging. Allow the drawings to dry.

Have children sit in a circle. Open your Bible to John 2:1-11, and show children the passage. Say: **This story tells about the very first miracle Jesus performed. He turned water into wine at a wedding banquet.**

Ask:

• **What is a miracle?**

• **Do you think the people at the wedding believed that Jesus could turn water into wine? Why or why not?**

• **Did you think you would be able to draw on the wet buttermilk? Why or why not?**

Have children tell about a miracle that has happened to them or someone they know. Then say: **Take your picture home as a reminder of something that seemed impossible but really was possible. God can work miracles in your life even when it seems impossible.**

Close in prayer, thanking God for working miracles in our lives.

JOHN 2:13-22

THEME:

Worship is important to God.

SUMMARY:

Use this creative storytelling activity to teach children about Jesus in the Temple with the merchants.

PREPARATION:

You'll need a Bible.

Open your Bible to John 2:13-22, and show children the passage. Say: **This is the story of Jesus in the Temple. I need you to help me act out the story.** Read the following rhyme to the children and help them act out the motions.

Jesus went on his way *(walk in place),*

To the Temple in Jerusalem to pray. *(Fold hands and bow head.)*

Jesus went to worship his Lord, dear *(bow with arms extended),*

Because Passover, the holiday, was near. *(Sweep arm from left to right over your head.)*

At the Temple, the merchants

were there *(look surprised and point finger at the floor)*,

But they had not come to say their prayers. *(Shake finger back and forth.)*

These men were there to sell *(motion people to come)*

And make money to live quite well. *(Rub fingers to thumbs on both hands.)*

When Jesus saw the merchants there *(shade eyes with hand)*,

He said, "Get out! My house is dear. *(Point away from body.)*

My father's house is not for this," *(point and shake finger side to side)*

As he threw out a merchant's pricing list. *(Pretend to throw away a piece of paper.)*

Jesus turned over the tables and chairs *(pretend to turn over imaginary tables)*

And turned the Temple back to a house of prayer. *(Make praying hands.)*

"My God will not like what you've done. *(Shake head back and forth.)*

Now gather your things and run." *(Point finger and extend arm away from body.)*

Jesus said, "This is God's special place," *(open hands slowly in front of body)*

As he looked at each merchant's face. *(Point finger to each "merchant.")*

"We worship and honor God here *(fold hands in prayer)*,

For our Lord is precious and dear. *(Cross arms across chest.)*

Worship is important to God," *(extend one arm up and look up)*

Jesus said, with a smile and a nod. *(Smile; nod again.)*

The merchants, they all went away. *(Run in place.)*

Then Jesus went inside to pray. *(Fold hands, bow head.)*

Say: It made Jesus very sad to see people doing other things inside the church where they should be worshipping and praying. God's church should be a place where we can worship him with prayer and singing and by praising him in many different ways.

JOHN 3:12-21

THEME:

Jesus came to save us.

SUMMARY:

Use this learning game to teach children that God loves us and sent his Son to save us.

PREPARATION:

You'll need a Bible and building blocks.

Open your Bible to John 3:12-21, and show the passage to the children. Say: **The Bible tells us that Jesus came so everyone who believes in him could live with him in heaven someday. God loves the world so much that he sent his Son, Jesus. Jesus came to save us.**

Explain to the children that our sins keep us from being free. It's as if our sins put us in jail. Jesus forgives our sins. It's as if he sets us free from jail. Jesus saves us.

Choose a child to pretend to be in jail, and have several children use blocks to build a pretend jail around that child. Choose another child to pretend to be Jesus. Have the child playing the part of Jesus pretend to unlock an imaginary door to let the jailed child go free. Then have all the children chant this rhyme.

One, two three,
Thanks to Jesus,
[Name of child in "jail"] **is free!**

Have the "free" child knock over the blocks. Then have the children change roles and repeat the game. Ask:

• **How does it feel to be set free from the jail?**

• **Why do you think God sent Jesus?**

• **What does Jesus set you free from?**

Close in prayer thanking God for sending his Son to set us free.

JOHN 3:16

THEME:

Jesus is the greatest gift.

SUMMARY:

Use this quiet reflection activity to teach children that God loves us so much that he sent his Son Jesus to love and teach us.

PREPARATION:

You'll need a Bible and a small beanbag.

Have the children sit in a circle Hold up the beanbag, and say: **In this game, we'll toss this beanbag to each other. When you catch the beanbag, finish this sentence, "I show someone love when I..."** You **might say that you show someone love by bringing them a drink, helping them clean up, feeding the cat, or saying nice words to them. Ready?**

Begin the game by completing the sentence, "I show someone love when I..." then gently toss the beanbag to a child. You may need to offer ideas or encourage children to help each other think of ways to show love. When everyone has had a turn, hold the beanbag and ask:

• **How do you feel when you show someone love?**

• **What are some ways that people show they love you?**

• **How do you feel when someone shows love to you?**

Say: **The Bible tells us that God loved us so much that he gave us Jesus.** Open your Bible to John 3:16, show children the passage, and read it aloud. **God loves us and sent Jesus. Just as we show others how much we love them, God showed his love by sending Jesus. Because God sent Jesus to love and teach us, we can live with God forever! Jesus is the greatest gift!**

Close in prayer, thanking God for loving us so much and giving us the gift of his Son Jesus.

JOHN 4:1-30

THEME:

Jesus' love is for everyone.

SUMMARY:

Use this creative storytelling activity to teach children that Jesus loves everyone no matter who they are or what they've done, just like the Samaritan woman at the well.

PREPARATION:

You'll need a Bible.

Say: **Today we're going to act out the story of the woman at the well.** Open your Bible to John 4:1-30 and show children the passage. Have kids stand and repeat your actions while you say the words.

One day, Jesus was traveling to a place called Galilee. *(Walk in place.)*

When he got tired, Jesus passed by a Samaritan city and decided to sit by a well and rest. *(Sit down and put your head on your hands.)*

A Samaritan woman saw Jesus when she came to draw some water out of the well. *(Pretend to pull water out of a well.)*

Jesus said to the woman, "I would like a drink!" *(Pretend to drink from a cup.)*

The Samaritan woman said, "Why are you talking to me? Jewish people don't even speak to people from Samaria." *(Raise your hands as if to ask a question.)*

Jesus said to her, "If you knew who I really am, you would ask me for a glass of water and I would give you special living water." *(Pretend to drink from a cup.)*

The Samaritan woman didn't understand. She asked, "How could you give me water? You don't have a bucket, and the well is very deep!" *(Pretend to peer down the well.)*

Jesus said, "The water from this well is regular water. If you drink it, you'll get thirsty again. But the water I have will bubble up like a fountain of eternal life— you'll never be thirsty again."

The Samaritan woman liked the sound of that! *(Clap your hands.)*

She said, "Sir, please give me some of this water so that I will never be thirsty again!" *(Shake your head.)*

Then Jesus told her to go get her husband and come back to the well. *(Point away from yourself then beckon with your hand.)*

The woman said she wasn't married, and Jesus said that she was honest. *(Shake your head "no," then smile.)*

The woman said, "You must be a prophet because you knew I wasn't married even before I told you." Jesus told the woman that he was the Messiah, the Son of God. *(Make a cross in the air.)*

Then the Samaritan woman went to the city to tell everyone what had happened. *(Run in place with your hands beside your mouth.)*

Ask:

• How can we tell others about Jesus?

• Why is it important to tell others about Jesus?

Close in prayer, thanking God for the love of his Son Jesus, and asking him to help us tell others about Jesus' love.

JOHN 5:1-18

THEME:

We can reach out to God.

SUMMARY:

Use this object lesson to teach children about the healing of the lame man at the pool of Bethesda.

PREPARATION:

You'll need a Bible, a child's wading pool or a large dishpan, and a two-liter bottle filled with small treats.

Before the activity, select an outside spot to place the wading pool or dishpan filled with water. Have the children stand an equal distance from the pool.

Open the Bible to John 5:1-18, and show children the passage. Say: **In this Bible story, people who couldn't walk wanted to get to the water in this pool as soon as it started swirling. They thought if they got in the pool, the water would heal them. When you see me swirl the water in the pool with the bottle, get to the pool as quickly as you can without walking. You can crawl, wriggle, roll, or scoot; but you can't stand on your feet. When you get to the pool, put one hand in the water and hold the other hand up to me.**

Swirl the pool water with the bottle. When all the children have gotten to the pool, pour one of the treats from the bottle into each child's hand. Ask:

• **Which hand got the treat, the one in the water or the one reaching out to me?**

• **How did it feel to get a treat? Why?**

Say: **It was Jesus who healed the man, not the water in the pool. Just like you got the treat by reaching out to me, the people who couldn't walk were healed when they reached out to Jesus.**

Ask:

• **How do you think the people felt when Jesus healed them?**

• **How do you think God feels when we reach out to him?**

Repeat the activity several times, encouraging the children to use different movements to get to the pool each time. Close in prayer, thanking God that he is here for us when we reach out to him.

JOHN 6:1-13

THEME:

Jesus wants us to share.

SUMMARY:

Use this creative storytelling idea to teach children about the boy who shared the five loaves and two fishes.

PREPARATION:

You'll need a Bible, small paper cups, and fish-shaped crackers.

Gather children together and say: **The Bible tells us about many times when Jesus shared meals with his disciples. Sometimes they ate breakfast together, sometimes they ate lunch, and sometimes they ate dinner together.**

Ask:

• **What's your favorite meal of the day? Why?**

• **What's your favorite food?**

Give each child a small paper cup filled with fish-shaped crackers. Say: **I'm thinking of a special lunch the Bible tells us about. Listen carefully while I read the story. Every time you hear me say the words "bread" or "fish," eat a cracker.**

Open the Bible to John 6:1-13, show children the passage, and read it aloud. Prompt children every time you say "bread" or "fish." Afterward, say: **Jesus made wonderful things happen when the little boy shared his lunch. And Jesus can make wonderful things happen when we share too.**

Ask:

• **Why does Jesus want us to share with others?**

• **What kinds of things can we share?**

Lead children in this rhyming prayer:

Five barley loaves and two small fishes,

The boy shared all he had.

Help us, Jesus, to share with others,

Because it makes you glad.

Amen.

JOHN 6:5-15

THEME:

God provides for our needs.

SUMMARY:

Use this finger play to teach children about Jesus feeding the five thousand.

PREPARATION:

You'll need a Bible.

Open your Bible to John 6:5-15, show children the passage, and paraphrase the story. Say: **God provided for all those people from one little boy sharing his lunch. Let's learn a rhyme to help us remember that God provides for us.**

Once one wee boy showed he did care *(hold out hand to show the height of a small child),*

He gave his lunch for all to share. *(Hold out hands.)*

Five small loaves and two small fishes *(hold up five left-hand* *fingers and two right-hand fingers)*,

"**Mmm, mmm, mmm! How delicious!**" *(Rub tummy.)*

Then Jesus took that one small lunch *(hold hands out as though taking something)*,

And made it feed oh such a bunch. *(Extend arms wide.)*

Lots of loaves and lots of fishes *(pretend to stack food with right hand)*,

"**Mmm, mmm, mmm! How delicious!**" *(Rub tummy.)*

JOHN 9:1-12

THEME:

Jesus can heal the wounds of our world.

SUMMARY:

Use this creative prayer to teach children to ask Jesus to heal their world.

PREPARATION:

You'll need a Bible, a red marker, a large world map, and plastic bandages.

Have the children form a circle, and place the map in the middle. Briefly talk about places where poverty, war, or violence abound.

Use a red marker to put a dot on each country or area you mention.

Open your Bible to John 9:1-12, show children the passage, and tell children a paraphrase of this story of Jesus healing the man born blind.

Say: **Just as Jesus healed the blind man, he can heal the wounds of our world. Let's pray right now.**

Distribute plastic bandages. Have children take turns sticking their bandages to the map, as you lead them in the following prayer.

Pray: **Dear God, we know we live in a broken world. Please heal the pain and suffering of people in our country and people who are far away. Just as you allowed the blind man to see, allow us to see you heal our world. In Jesus' name, amen.**

JOHN 10:14

THEME:

Our heavenly identity comes from Jesus.

SUMMARY:

Use this object lesson to teach children that God knows us so well that he even knows how many hairs are on our heads.

PREPARATION:

You'll need a Bible, a birth certificate, a driver's license, and a library card.

Have children sit in a circle. Show them each piece of identification. Say: **Identification cards are important because they tell important information. I have to have my driver's license with me every time I drive. It tells other people who I am and that I can drive. You don't have a driver's license yet, but each of you has a birth certificate. When you were born, your parents were given your birth certificate to show who you are. When we go to the library, we have to have our library cards so we can check out books. It tells the librarian who we are.**

Ask:

• **When we get to heaven, what kind of identification do you think we'll need?**

Open your Bible to John 10:14, show children the passage, and read it aloud. Say: **That means that Jesus knows each one of us so well. In fact, we are so well-known that the Bible tells us that God even knows how many hairs we have on our heads. Our heavenly identity comes from Jesus knowing who we are.**

Ask:

• **If God knows how many hairs we have, what else do you think he knows about us?**

• **How do you feel about God knowing you so well?**

Close with prayer, thanking God for identifying us as his children.

JOHN 10:27

THEME:

We are Jesus' sheep.

SUMMARY:

Use this craft idea to teach children that Jesus wants us to follow him.

PREPARATION:

You'll need a Bible, cardboard,

scissors, cotton balls, glue, and large craft sticks.

Before the activity, cut out a lamb-shape mask from cardboard for each child. Cut a hole in the center of the mask big enough for the child's face.

Give each child a lamb mask. Have children each glue cotton balls around the entire mask front. Then help children each glue a large craft stick to the bottom of the mask for a handle.

Have children sit in a circle with their masks. Open your Bible to John 10:27, show children the passage, and read it aloud. Say: **Jesus tells us in this verse that his sheep follow and obey him. We are like Jesus' sheep. He takes care of us. We make Jesus happy when we follow and obey him.**

Ask:

• **Why does Jesus feel happy when we follow and obey him?**

• **What are some ways we can obey Jesus?**

Have children hold up their sheep masks as you lead them in the following song to the tune of "The Wheels on the Bus Go Round and Round."

> **I am one of Jesus' sheep,**
> **Jesus' sheep,**
> **Jesus' sheep.**
> **I am one of Jesus' sheep,**
> **And I will follow him.**

JOHN 11:25

THEME:
Jesus' love never runs out.

SUMMARY:
Use this object lesson to teach children that we can live a full life in Jesus if we believe in him.

PREPARATION:
You'll need a Bible, a box of cookies, and an empty cookie box.

Have children sit in a circle. Pretend to eat cookies from the empty cookie box. Say: **These are good cookies. I'm going to share these cookies. When I pass around the box, take a cookie.**

Pass around the empty box. Ask:

• **Why aren't you getting any cookies?**

Say: **This box was filled with cookies earlier.**

Ask:

• How did it make you feel to think you were getting cookies only to find out they were all gone?

Say: There's someone who's always full of love for us. His love never runs out. Open the Bible to John 11:25, show children the passage, and read it aloud. Jesus died for us because he loves us and want us to live in heaven with him someday. When you believe in Jesus, he's always with you. Hold up the empty cookie box. Instead of living an empty life like the empty cookie box, with Jesus we can have a full life like this full box of cookies. Hold up the full box of cookies.

Let's pray and thank God for giving us a full life in his Son Jesus, and then I'll share these cookies with you.

After you lead children in prayer, distribute the cookies. As children fill their tummies, have them think of ways they can ask God to fill their hearts.

JOHN 11:35

THEME:

Jesus understands our feelings.

SUMMARY:

Use this creative prayer to teach children to give their worries and concerns to God.

PREPARATION:

You'll need a Bible, facial tissues, and an empty tissue box.

Gather children around you. Give each child a tissue, and say: When we're sad, we use tissues to wipe away our tears.

Ask:

• What are some things that might make us cry?

Open your Bible to John 11:35, show children the passage, and read it aloud. Ask:

• Have you ever thought about Jesus crying?

• What would it be like to see Jesus crying?

• What things make Jesus sad?

Say: Jesus cried because he was sad that his close friend Lazarus was dead. But Jesus also cried because he knew how sad Lazarus' sisters and friends were. Jesus cares for our hurts too. When we're sad, Jesus is sad for us.

I want you to think of one thing that makes you sad. Then we're going to pass around this box. When the box comes to you, place your tissue in the box, and remember that Jesus wants to wipe away your tears.

After you have passed around the empty tissue box and the children have put in their tissues, teach children the words to this rhyming prayer:

Thank you, Jesus, that when I cry,

You're there to dry my tears.

You're always with me when I'm sad.

You take away my fears.

Amen.

JOHN 13:2-17

THEME:

Jesus wants us to serve others.

SUMMARY:

Use this service idea to teach children that Jesus washed his disciples' feet to show us how to serve others.

PREPARATION:

You'll need a Bible and enough baby wipes for each child to have one.

Have children sit in a circle. Open your Bible to John 13:2-17, and show children the passage. Say: **This is the story of Jesus washing his disciples' feet. In Jesus' day, people wore sandals and walked everywhere. Their feet got tired, dusty, and dirty. Washing feet was a job that servants did. But Jesus washed the feet of his disciples to show us that because he was willing to serve others, we should serve others too.**

Ask:

• **What are some ways we can serve others?**

• **How do you think Jesus feels when we serve others? Why?**

Have children put their feet out in front of them. Place the container of baby wipes in the center of the circle. Choose one child to be the first foot washer. Say: **Today we're going to wipe each other's shoes to help us remember that Jesus wants us to serve each other.**

Teach the children the following rhyme:

One foot, two feet,

Inside-your-shoes feet,

[Foot washer's name] **wants to serve you,**

As Jesus showed us how.

Have the foot washer walk around behind the children as they say the rhyme and stop on the word "how." Then have the foot washer and the child he or she stopped behind go to the center of the circle. Have the foot washer take a baby wipe and wipe the shoes of the second child. The foot washer will then take the place of the child he or she has served, and the child who has been served will be the new foot washer. (Note: The first foot washer will return to the circle with his or her feet still dirty.) When the second child returns to the circle, have him or her sit cross-legged to show the others that his or her feet have already been washed. If the new foot washer stops behind a child who is sitting cross-legged, he or she should proceed to the next child who still has his or her legs extended. Continue until all children have been served.

JOHN
13:34

THEME:

God commands us to love others.

SUMMARY:

Use this devotion idea to teach children that we are to love others as God loves us.

PREPARATION:

You'll need a Bible, a large red paper heart with the words "Love one another" printed on it, and an empty brown medicine bottle. For each child you'll also need a small red paper heart printed with "Love one another" on it attached to a piece of string to form a necklace.

Have children sit in a circle. Ask:
• **Has anyone ever said or done something to you that made you feel sad? hurt? angry? afraid?**
• **How did that make you feel?**
Say: **When people hurt our feelings, we have a hard time liking those people. But God commands us to love everyone.**

Open your Bible to John 13:34, show children the passage, and read it aloud. Hold up the large paper heart. Say: **God tells us that we are to love one another just as he loves us.**

Ask:
• **How can we show God's love to others?**
• **When might it be hard to share God's love?**
Say: **We may not always like what other people say or do, but we must love them. It reminds me of taking medicine when I'm sick.**

Hold up the medicine bottle.
Say: **Sometimes I may not want to swallow hard-to-take medicine, but I know I need it to get better.**

It's the same with loving hard-to-get-along-with people. **God has commanded us to love them, and I feel better when I obey him. I still may not like what they do or say, but, with God's help, I can show his love to them.**

Give each child a paper heart necklace to serve as a reminder of God's command to love other people as God loves us. Close with the following prayer:

Dear God, we know that in this world others will do and say things that we don't like or things that might even hurt us or our feelings. Help us love them as you have commanded us to do. Amen.

JOHN 14:6

THEME:

Jesus is the way.

SUMMARY:

Use this object lesson to teach children that the only way to heaven is through Jesus.

PREPARATION:

You'll need a Bible and a plastic shape-sorter toy with a circle shape and diamond, star, and circle holes.

Before class, draw a face on the circle shape.

Have children sit in a circle. Show children the shape sorter and the circle-shape face. Say: **This puzzle is probably pretty easy for you to do. Let's pretend that this circle shape is a person. This person wants to get to heaven. This person decides, "I'll be a star at doing good things to get to heaven."**

Have a child try to push the circle shape through the star hole. Ask:

• **Can the circle say, "I'll buy my way into heaven"?**

Have another child try to push the circle shape through the diamond hole. Say: **Those are silly ideas! There's only one way for the circle to get into the shape-sorter.**

Ask:

• **What is the only way the circle can get into the shape sorter?**

Have another child push the circle shape through the circle hole. Then open your Bible to John 14:6, show children the passage, and read it aloud. Ask:

• **How do we get to our Father in heaven?**

Say: **We must go through Jesus. It's that simple—just like the shape-sorter puzzle is simple. One shape, one hole. One person,** one way to heaven. **Jesus is the only way.**

JOHN 15:1-5

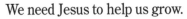

THEME:
We need Jesus to help us grow.

SUMMARY:
Use this prayer idea to teach children that we bloom with Jesus living in and through us.

PREPARATION:
You'll need a Bible; a medium- to large-sized plant; scissors or pruning shears; and gardening items such as a trowel, a watering can, seed packets, an apron, gloves, and rubber boots.

Before the activity, set out the gardening items on the floor in the center of the sitting circle.

Have children sit in a circle around the gardening items. Ask:

• **What could we use these items for?**

• **What does a gardener do?**

Say: **If I trim this plant, it might look like it hurts the plant.**

Snip off one of the branches, leaves, or vines.

Say: **But it doesn't because pruning helps plants to grow thicker, stronger, and fuller.**

Set the plant down, and hold up the part you cut off. Ask:

• **If this branch lays here on its own, what will happen to it?**

Say: **The branch will dry up and die. It needs nourishment to grow because it is part of the plant.**

Open your Bible to John 15:1-5, show children the passage, and read it aloud. Say: **In this passage Jesus told his friends, "I am the vine; you are the branches." This means that we need Jesus to help us grow. As we grow in Jesus, he will help us to branch out and touch other people with his love.**

Show children the potted plant.

Say: **Plants and flowers around us can remind us of the life we have because of Jesus and his love for us. We'll use this plant in our prayer time as we thank God for the many blessings he gives to us. I will start the prayer, and then I'll pass the plant to the person on my right. When you get the plant, say a thank-you prayer and pass the plant to the person beside you.**

Pray: **Dear God, thank you for loving me just as I am.**

Pass the plant to the child on your right, and have children continue praying and passing the plant until it goes around the whole circle. Close with everyone saying: **Amen**.

JOHN 21:4-17

THEME:

Jesus forgives our sins.

SUMMARY:

Use this creative storytelling idea to teach children that Jesus forgave Peter and that Jesus forgives us, too.

PREPARATION:

You'll need a Bible.

Open your Bible to John 21:4-17, and show children the passage. Say: **This Bible story is about a time Jesus appeared to his friends after he rose from the dead.**

Have the children join you in doing the italicized motions throughout the story.

Say: **After Jesus died and rose again, he appeared to his disciples many times. Each time they saw Jesus, the disciples were amazed that he'd actually risen from the dead.**

One evening, Peter, Thomas, Nathanael, and some of Jesus' other friends went fishing. They got into a boat and rowed out into the Sea of Galilee. Let's pretend we're in the boat with Jesus' friends. *(Form pairs, and have partners sit facing each other so the bottoms of their feet are touching. Then show children how to hold hands and rock back and forth as if they're rowing.)*

After the men found a good fishing spot, they cast their nets into the water, hoping to catch lots of tasty fish. *(Pretend to toss a large net into the water.)* **When the men pulled the nets in** *(pretend to pull in a net)*, **there wasn't a single fish! All night they tossed their nets into the water** *(continue to cast and then pull in a net)*, **but they didn't catch anything.**

Just as dawn was casting its yellow light over the water, the disciples heard a voice calling them from the shore.

"Friends," the man called, "haven't you caught any fish?"

The men shook their heads. "No," they replied, "not even one!" *(Shake your head "no.")*

Then the man on the shore called to them, "Throw your net out from the right side of the boat, and you'll find some fish."

The men sighed. It had been a long night, and they were tired. *(Yawn and stretch.)* **Did this**

stranger really think they'd catch anything now? But it couldn't hurt, so the disciples tossed their net once more, this time on the right side of the boat. *(Pretend to toss a net to your right.)*

Suddenly, the net became so heavy that it was about to break! All the men had to help to pull in the net! *(Pretend to pull in the heavy net.)* The net was so full of fish that the men couldn't even pull it into the boat! They dragged it behind them as they rowed back to shore. *(Pretend to row again with your partner.)* When the disciples got to the shore, they discovered that the stranger who had talked to them was Jesus!

They all gathered for a fish breakfast there on the sandy beach. After they ate, Jesus asked Peter, "Do you truly love me more than anything?"

"Yes, Lord," Peter said. "You know I love you."

Then Jesus asked again, "Do you truly love me?"

Again Peter answered, "Yes, Lord. You know that I love you."

A third time, Jesus asked Peter, "Do you love me?"

Peter felt bad that Jesus asked him three times. But Peter remembered that three times he'd said he didn't know Jesus.

"Lord, you know everything; you know I love you."

Jesus forgave Peter for saying he didn't know him. Jesus wanted Peter to remember how important it is to love him with all your heart.

When we do bad things, Jesus forgives us, too. Let's tell Jesus how much we love him right now.

Close by having children say simple, one-sentence prayers.

Acts

*"Therefore let all Israel be assured of this:
God has made this Jesus, whom you
crucified, both Lord and Christ."*

Acts 2:36

ACTS
2:1-21

THEME:

God gave us the Holy Spirit.

SUMMARY:

Use this snack to teach children about God giving the disciples the Holy Sprit at Pentecost.

PREPARATION:

You'll need a Bible, small trays or dishes of red and brown (a mixture of red and green) food coloring, large marshmallows, cotton swabs, toothpicks, and graham crackers.

Open your Bible to Acts 2:1-21, and show children the passage. Say: **Today's Bible story tells us about the time God sent the Holy Spirit. Jesus' disciples were together in a special room in Jerusalem. There were crowds of people in the streets because it was the feast of Pentecost. People came from all over the world to attend the celebration.**

While the disciples were praying, they heard a strange sound. It was the sound of a great wind. It grew louder and louder, and it filled the house where they were praying. **The disciples looked at each other, and they saw what looked like little fiery flames sitting on the top of each person's head!**

God knew that the disciples couldn't see the Holy Spirit, so he sent the wind so they could hear it and feel it, and the flames of fire so they could see it. God gave them the Holy Spirit to be their teacher and friend and to help them tell others about him. That day, the Holy Spirit gave the disciples the power to speak to thousands of people in their own languages. Lots and lots of people believed in Jesus that day.

Give each child two large marshmallows, half a cotton swab, and three toothpicks. Say: **We're going to make a special treat to celebrate that God sent the Holy Spirit.**

Have the children use a toothpick to connect their marshmallows. Then have them paint faces on their marshmallow "disciples" by dipping the end of a toothpick in the brown food coloring. Have them push half a cotton swab into the top marshmallow so that the cotton is sticking out of the top. Push a toothpick through the bottom marshmallow to make arms. When all the children have made a snack, have them gather in a circle holding their snacks. Ask:

• **Who remembers our story**

and what happened to the disciples' heads when the Holy Spirit came?

After the children respond, allow them to dip the cotton swabs at the top of their "disciples" in the red food coloring. Show the children how to take their snack apart carefully to eat it. Provide graham crackers to go with the marshmallow disciples.

ACTS 2:44-45

THEME:

God wants us to give to others.

SUMMARY:

Use this service idea to teach children how to show others their love for Jesus.

PREPARATION:

You'll need a Bible, a small toy for each child, a CD of children's music, a CD player, tissue paper, tape, and ribbon.

Before the activity, contact the person in charge of your church nursery. Discuss the idea of having the preschool children give some of their own personal toys to the church nursery. Ask if there are any specific toy needs the nursery has.

Send a letter to your preschoolers' parents describing the project. Be sure to ask for toys that are clean and usable.

Have children sit in a large circle on the floor. Give each child a small toy. Say: **Each of you is holding a toy in your hand. We're going to use these toys to play a game called Musical Toys. When the music plays, pass the toy you are holding to the person next to you, and keep passing the toys around the circle until the music stops. When the music stops, stop passing the toys and hold on to the toy in your hand. When the music begins again, continue passing the toys around until the music stops again.**

Play the music and the game for a few minutes. Ask:

• **How did it feel to keep giving away toys that you wished you could keep?**

• **How do you think children that don't have any toys feel?**

Collect the toys and place them out of the way. Open your Bible to the book of Acts and show it to the children. Say: **I want to tell you a story about some people who lived a long time ago. This story is found in the Bible in the book of Acts. These people had just heard about how much Jesus loved them, and they wanted to show their love for Jesus in a special way.**

Ask:

• **How do you show other people how much you love Jesus?**

Read Acts 2:44-45 aloud. Say: **These people shared everything they had with other people who needed things. If someone had two pairs of shoes and another person didn't have any shoes, the person with the extra pair of shoes gave the second pair to the person who needed shoes. They also shared their food with each other.**

Ask:

• **What's your favorite toy to play with?**

• **How many of you have more than one toy?**

Say: **Our church has a nursery where the babies and children smaller than you play while their moms and dads go to church or to Sunday school. Some of you probably played there when you were smaller. We could be like the people we learned about in the Bible who shared everything they had. We could give some of our toys that we don't play with anymore to the children in the nursery. When you go home, see if you can find one toy at your house that you would be willing to give away to the children in the nursery. Bring the toys to class next week and we'll wrap the presents and deliver them to the nursery.**

The next week, help children wrap the toys they've brought in with tissue paper and ribbon. Then take the children to deliver the gifts to the nursery. If possible, allow some time for the preschoolers to help the nursery children open the gifts and play with them together.

Return to your classroom and close in prayer, thanking God for the children and their willingness to share. Thank the children for their generosity to the children in the church nursery and for showing their love for Jesus.

ACTS 3:1-8

THEME:

Help others as you are able.

SUMMARY:

Use this travel idea to teach children about Peter and John healing the crippled man at the Temple gate.

PREPARATION:

You'll need a Bible, trash bags, a pen or pencil, paper, hand soap, and paper towels.

Before the activity, recruit some adult helpers for this activity. Arrange for a leader in your church to come to your classroom at the end of the activity to receive the repair list from the children.

Open your Bible to Acts 3:1-8, and show children the passage. Say: **This Bible passage tells us about two men named Peter and John. One day, they were traveling to the Temple to tell people about God. When they got to the gate of the Temple, they saw a poor man who couldn't walk, sitting on a mat. He was asking for money to buy food. Peter and John had no money to** give to the man, but Peter knew what to do. He could help the man through the power of Jesus. Peter said, "In the name of Jesus Christ of Nazareth, walk." The man got up and walked! He was healed! The man began praising and thanking God.

Ask:

• **Why does God want us to help others?**

• **When we don't have money to bring to church, what are some other ways we can help?**

Say: **God wants us to be helpful to others, just like Peter and John were helpful. Today we're going to help others by traveling around our church to help keep it clean and find things that need to be fixed. We'll go outside and pick up the trash we find, and we'll make a list of anything that needs to be repaired. Then we'll travel back to our room, and we'll give the list of what needs to be fixed to one of our church leaders.**

Distribute trash bags, and take the children outside. Help children pick up trash and look for any repairs to list. For example, your list may include items such as mend fence, cut grass, clean flower bed, or repair playground equipment.

When you return to your room, have children wash their hands. Have your church leader come to your room for the children to present the repair list.

ACTS 9:23-25

THEME:
God wants us to help others.

SUMMARY:
Use this song to teach children that Saul's friends helped him when he was in danger.

PREPARATION:
You'll need a Bible.

Open your Bible to Acts 9:23-25 and show children the passage. Say: **This passage tells about how Saul's friends helped him when he was in danger. God wants us to help others too.**

Ask:

• **Why do you think God wants us to help others?**

Say: **Let's learn a song to help us remember to help others.** Lead children in the words and motions to this song, sung to the tune of "The Farmer in the Dell."

Let's give a helping hand *(wiggle hands)*
To anyone we can. *(Point around the room.)*
Here's my right hand, here's my left *(raise right hand, then left hand)*;
Let's give a helping hand. *(Wiggle hands.)*

Let's give a kind word too *(move hands like a puppet mouth)*,
When our friends feel blue. *(Make a sad face.)*
A kind word always shows we care. *(Hug self.)*
Let's give a kind word too. *(Move hands like a puppet mouth.)*

Let's give with hearts of love *(make a heart shape on chest with pointer fingers)*,
Good news from God above. *(Point to heaven.)*
Jesus came to save us all. *(Put arms around each other.)*
Let's give with hearts of love. *(Make a heart shape on chest with pointer fingers.)*

ACTS
9:26-28

THEME:
Turn your life around and follow Jesus.

SUMMARY:
Use this song to teach children that Barnabas helped Saul turn his life around to follow Jesus.

PREPARATION:
You'll need a Bible.

Open your Bible to Acts 9:26-28, and read the passage aloud. Say: **People were afraid of Saul because he was mean to Jesus. But Barnabas helped Saul learn to follow Jesus. It makes God very happy when we follow Jesus. Jesus will help us turn our lives around just like he turned Saul's life around.**

Lead children in singing this song to the tune of "Hokey Pokey."

> **You put your** [right hand] **in** *(put your right hand in the circle)*,
> **You put your** [right hand] **out** *(put your right hand outside the circle)*,
> **You put your** [right hand] **in and you shake it all about.** *(Put your hand into the middle of the circle and shake it.)*
> **You want to follow Jesus so you turn your life around.** *(Turn in place.)*
> **That's what it's all about.** *(Clap on each word.)*

Sing additional verses substituting left hand, right leg, left leg, head, and whole self.

Ask:
• **How can we follow Jesus?**
• **How does it make Jesus feel when we follow him?**

Say: **Just as Barnabas helped Saul follow Jesus, Jesus will help us follow him too.**

ACTS
14:17

THEME:
God is faithful in providing for our needs.

SUMMARY:
Use this craft idea to teach children that God gives us what we need because he loves us.

PREPARATION:
You'll need a Bible, aluminum foil or tinsel, tape, cotton balls, glue, white envelopes, a hole

punch, yarn, scissors, and paper towels.

Before the activity, cut aluminum foil into ½x6-inch strips.

Give each child an envelope and paper towel. Have children crumple the towels and stuff them into their envelopes to make clouds. Show children how to lick the envelope flaps and stick tinsel or foil "raindrops" on the adhesive before folding the flaps down. Tape any raindrops that won't stick. Have children glue cotton balls onto the sealed envelope flaps to make fluffy rain clouds.

As each child finishes, punch holes at each end of the envelope top. String a length of yarn about ten inches long through the holes. Knot the ends of the yarn and let the child swirl the rain cloud through the air.

Have children sit in a circle with their rain clouds. Open your Bible to Acts 14:17, show children the passage, and read it aloud. Say: **This tells us that God shows us he is faithful by providing things we need like rain to water the earth, food to fill our tummies, and joy to fill our hearts.**

Ask:

• **Why do we need the rain?**

• **Why is God faithful in providing what we need?**

Say: **God is faithful to us because he loves us. Every time we see the rain, we can remember God's faithfulness.**

As children swirl their rain clouds, lead them in singing this rainy-day song to the tune of "The Farmer in the Dell."

> **Drippity-drippa-drop.**
> **Drippity-drippa-drop.**
> **Rain is falling from the clouds.**
> **I hope it never stops!**

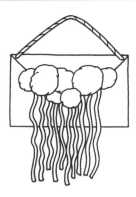

ACTS 16:22-28

THEME:
Praise God in all things.

SUMMARY:
Use this learning song to teach children that God is always with us.

PREPARATION:
You'll need a Bible.

Open your Bible to Acts 16:22-28, and show children the passage. Tell children a paraphrase of the story. Ask:

• **What did Paul and Silas do when they were in jail?**

Say: **Paul and Silas could have been mad or afraid in jail but they sang and praised God. We, too, can sing praises to God because he is always with us, even when something scary happens.**

Have two people form a bridge by holding hands. Then have other children line up and walk under the bridge while singing this song to the tune of "London Bridge."

Paul and Silas preached the Word,
Preached the Word,
Preached the Word.
Paul and Silas preached the Word,
But they got thrown in jail.
(Have the bridge lower and capture a child.)

Praising God will set them free,
Set them free,
Set them free. *(Rock child back and forth in the lowered bridge.)*
Praising God will set them free,
They got the victory! *(Open bridge.)*

Repeat the song, having children continue to walk under the bridge until each child has been "captured."

ACTS 17:24

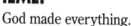

THEME:
God made everything.

SUMMARY:
Use this creative dance to teach children that God made the whole world and everything in it.

PREPARATION:
You'll need a Bible and a drum or rhythm instrument.

Have children sit in a circle. Open your Bible to Acts 17:24, show children the passage, and read it aloud. Ask:

• **What wonderful things did God make?**

Say: **God made everything you see in nature. He made the highest mountains and the lowest valleys. God made the sun, the clouds, and the rivers. God made everything, and we're going to learn a dance to celebrate what God has made.**

Stand in a circle, and have

someone beat the drum slowly and rhythmically. Lead children in walking in a circle, taking one step on each drumbeat. Chant these words, while leading children in the dance motions:

God made the mountains. *(Walk to the right on tiptoes while touching your fingertips together to create a "peak" over your head.)*

God made the valleys. *(Bend over and walk to the left, clasping your hands below you to form a V.)*

God made the clouds up in the sky. *(Stop walking, turn around in place, and make swirling motions overhead.)*

God made the sun that shines so warm. *(Face into the circle, and touch the tips of your fingers together to form a "sun" overhead.)*

God made the rivers. *(Wiggle hands, and walk toward the middle of the circle.)*

God made you and me. *(Join hands, and crouch down.)*

Thank you, God! *(Stand up, still holding hands.)*

Repeat the activity, letting children take turns beating the drum.

ROMANS

"Therefore, since we have been justified through faith, we have peace with God through our Lord Jesus Christ."

Romans 5:1

ROMANS 1:16a

THEME:
We are proud to follow Jesus.

SUMMARY:
Use this song to teach children that we are proud of the gospel and not ashamed to follow Jesus.

PREPARATION:
You'll need a Bible.

Open your Bible to Romans 1:16a, and show children the passage. Say: **This verse tells us about the time that Paul announced that he was not ashamed of the gospel. That means he was proud of God's Word and proud to follow Jesus.**

Lead children in singing this song to the tune of "Did You Ever See a Lassie?"

I'm proud to follow Jesus,
Yes, Jesus; oh, Jesus.
I'm proud to follow Jesus,
Wherever he goes.

I'm not ashamed of Jesus,
Yes, Jesus; oh, Jesus.
I'm not ashamed of Jesus,
I'm proud he's my friend.

Ask:
• **What makes you proud about knowing Jesus?**
• **How do you think Jesus feels when we are proud to follow him?**
• **How can we show others that we follow Jesus?**

Close in prayer, thanking Jesus for being our friend, and ask him to help us tell others of his love.

ROMANS 1:20a

THEME:
God is invisible, yet we know he exists.

SUMMARY:
Use this devotion idea to teach children that we know God exists because of the things he has made.

PREPARATION:
You'll need a Bible; a blow-dryer with a cool setting; and a Ping-Pong ball, balloon, or small beach ball. For extra fun, decorate the ball to look like planet Earth.

Have children sit in a circle. Ask:
• **What are some things you can't see but you know are there?**

Say: **Some powerful, invisible things I know of are germs, sound, and wind. A strong gust of wind is invisible, but it can knock a big truck on its side.**

Turn the blow-dryer on cool, and point it straight up. Put the Ping-Pong ball (or balloon or beach ball) in the stream of air until it's held up by the air. Ask:

• **Can you see air?**

• **How do we know the air is there?**

Have children each wave their hand over the airstream from the blow-dryer. Ask:

• **What happened when you waved your hand over the airstream?**

Say: **Just as the invisible airstream held up this Ping-Pong ball, our invisible God created the world around us. We can't see the air holding up the ball, but we know it's there. We can't see God, but we know he's there.**

Ask:

• **How do we know that God is there even though we can't see him?**

Open the Bible to Romans 1:20a, show children the passage, and read it aloud. Say: **This means that even though God is invisible, we know he exists because of the things he has made—the sun, the moon, the stars, and the animals. We**

know he is there because his power shines down on us as the warmth of the sun, and swirls around us as the wind. We know God is here with us, even though we can't see him.

Close with the following prayer:

Dear God, we are amazed at the things you have created. We can see, hear, and touch the world around us and understand what a wonderful creator you are. Thank you for the comfort of knowing that you are with us all the time. In Jesus' name, amen.

ROMANS 2:11

THEME:
We're all God's favorites.

SUMMARY:
Use this object lesson to teach children that God loves us all equally.

PREPARATION:
You'll need a Bible and a bag of multi-flavored candy such as Gummi Savers.

Have children sit in a circle. Say: **I have a bag of flavored**

candy here. Take one piece that is your favorite flavor.

Pass the candy around the circle and have children choose their favorite flavors.

Say: **Let's imagine that we threw all of you in a bag and offered God the chance to choose one of you. I wonder if he would pick through the bag saying things such as, "I don't like blue-eyed ones" "This one's too skinny" "I don't want that one, he's got dirt behind his ears" or "Now here's a sweet one with curly red hair and a big smile. I'll take this one."**

Ask:

• **Do you think God would say that? Why or why not?**

Open your Bible to Romans 2:11, show children the passage, and read it aloud. Say: **This passage tell us that God would look into the bag of kids, smile, and say, "I love them all" because he judges us all the same.**

Now, you might think you're better looking, better behaved, smarter, or nicer than your brother, sister, or your friend, but God does not show favoritism. He loves all of you equally.

Pass the bag of candy around the circle again. Have children close their eyes and take the first one they touch as they reach in the bag. Say: **You must be willing to eat that candy without any complaining. You don't have to take one. But if you do, you can't show favoritism just like God doesn't show favoritism.**

Let children eat the candy.

Say: **This week, be a friend to someone you normally wouldn't pick as a friend. God has already chosen to love that person as much as he loves you! Let's pray for a specific person that you'll try to be friends with this week.**

As you say the prayer, pause for a moment and have children fill in the name of the person they're praying for.

Pray: **Dear God, thank you for not choosing favorites. Help me to be friends with** (pause) **this week. I know that you love** (pause) **as much as you love me. In Jesus' name, amen.**

Give each child one more piece of candy to take home as a reminder to work on being friends with the person that he or she prayed about.

ROMANS 5:8

THEME:
Jesus died for us.

SUMMARY:
Use this object lesson to teach children that God sacrificed his Son so we could enjoy eternal life.

PREPARATION:
You'll need a Bible; a paper cup for each child filled with a different trail mix ingredient, such as peanuts (check for allergies), raisins, or chocolate chips; and a large bowl.

Gather children in a circle and say: **I've brought a special treat today. I'll pass it out, but don't eat yet.**

Distribute cups. Ask:

• **What did you get?**

• **What would happen if we put our snacks into this bowl?**

Have children pour their snacks in the bowl. Then mix. Ask:

• **Why were you willing to give up your treat?**

• **How does it feel to know others will enjoy a yummy snack because of what you gave up?**

Say: **God gave something special for us too.** Open your Bible to Romans 5:8, show children the passage, and read it aloud. **Because God loves us so much, he gave his Son Jesus so we could enjoy eternal life in heaven.**

Ask:

• **What are other ways God shows us he loves us?**

• **What are some ways we can show God we love him?**

Distribute cups of trail mix. Close in prayer, thanking God for the wonderful sacrifice he made for us.

ROMANS 6:6-7

THEME:
God forgives our sins.

SUMMARY:
Use this snack idea to teach children that God peels away our sins.

PREPARATION:
You'll need a Bible and a banana for each person.

Have children sit in a circle. Show children a banana. Ask:

• **What is this?**

• **What do I do with it?**

• **How do I open the banana?**

Say: **Oh, I see. I have to peel the banana to get to the sweet fruit inside.**

Open your Bible to Romans 6:6-7, show children the passage, and read it aloud. Say: **This means that when we sin or do something wrong, it's possible for us to be forgiven. All we have to do is ask God to forgive us and he peels away our sin. Just like we peel away the skin of a banana to get to the sweet fruit, God peels away our sin to make our hearts clean and pure.**

Give each child a banana. Have children each peel their banana and eat it. Ask:

• **How do you think God feels when we sin or do something wrong?**

• **Why do you think God wants to peel away our sins?**

• **What happens to our hearts when God takes away our sins?**

Close in the following prayer:

Thank you, God,

For peeling away our sins,

For cleansing our hearts,

And making us new from within.

Amen.

ROMANS 6:23

THEME:

God gives us eternal life.

SUMMARY:

Use this devotion idea to teach children that God's gift of eternal life is free.

PREPARATION:

You'll need a Bible and inexpensive items such as stickers, pencils, or candy.

Have children sit in a circle and place the gift items in the center of the circle. Ask:

• **What is a gift?**

• **What's the best thing about a gift?**

Say: **I have some gifts here for you. You may each choose one gift from the center of the circle.**

After each child has selected a gift, say: **If you chose a pencil, you owe me a nickel. If you chose a piece of candy, you owe me a dime. If you chose a sticker, you owe me a quarter.**

Ask:

• **If I were to make you pay for the gifts I gave you, would they really be gifts? Why or why not?**

Say: **You don't really have to pay me for these items. They are gifts I'm giving to you. Let's read in the Bible about another gift.**

Open your Bible to Romans 6:23, show children the passage, and read it aloud. Say: **This tells us that God has given us eternal life through his Son Jesus. That means that we can live forever with God in heaven. God's gift of eternal life is FREE! We can't do anything to earn it. God wants us to share his free gift of love.**

Close in prayer, thanking God for his love gift. Have children each take another gift from the gift assortment to give to a friend and tell about God's free gift of love to us!

ROMANS 8:38-39

THEME:
God is always with us.

SUMMARY:
Use this imaginary trip to teach children that no matter where we go, God is with us.

PREPARATION:
You'll need a Bible.

Have children sit in a circle. Say: **We're going to take a pretend trip to an amusement park.**

Ask:

• **What kinds of things will we see there?**

Have children pretend to climb on a bus and ride to the amusement park. Ham it up by pretending to go around curves and bumps. Then have children "climb" off the bus.

Say: **Hooray! We're here! Look over there; they have one of those radical, rip-roaring, razorback roller coaster rides! That thing is the highest, fastest, steepest, scariest, most powerful roller coaster ride I've ever seen! Let's ride it.**

Have children pretend to board the roller coaster and sit in a line in pairs as if on a roller coaster. Say the words and do the following motions with the children:

Sit down, and strap yourself in! Here we go! Up, up, up, up... *(Lean way back as you speak.)* **We're almost to the top! Are you ready for the big downhill? Hold your hands in the air, and be ready to scream! Here we go!** *(Scream with the children, then shout these instructions.)* **Lean to the left; now lean to the right; bounce up and down for the bumps—one, two, three! Now hang on tight, here comes**

the loop! We're going upside-down, so put your head between your legs! Now lean way back. Lean to the left again; now lean to the right. Bounce up and down for the last bump. Wow! We made it back. That was scary!

Pretend the roller coaster has come to a stop. Have children "climb" off and sit in a circle. Ask:

• **What scary thing has happened to you?**

• **What scary thing has happened to your family or friends?**

• **Do you think God is with us even when scary or awful things happen?**

Open your Bible to Romans 8:38-39, show children the passage, and read it aloud. Say: **This passage means that nothing can ever separate us from God's love.**

Ask:

• **Where can we go that God isn't with us?**

• **Is God with us when things are scary? Why?**

• **Is God with us even on a roller coaster? Why?**

Say: **Because God loves us so much, he is always with us.**

Teach children the words and motions to this rhyming prayer sung to the tune of "Row, Row, Row Your Boat."

Thanks for happy times *(raise your hands)*,

And excitement, too. *(Bounce up and down.)*

When the bumps come, help us pray *(fold hands as in prayer)*,

And hold on tight to you! *(Wrap arms around yourself as if holding someone close.)*

ROMANS 12:6a

THEME:

God made me special.

SUMMARY:

Use this affirmation idea to teach children that God gives us different gifts.

PREPARATION:

You'll need a Bible; and eight-inch thin, white paper circles.

Before the activity, cut thin, white paper into eight-inch circles. Cut two circles for each child. Cake-pan liners work well for this activity. (Note: Coffee filters will not work well for this project—they're difficult to tear.)

Help children fold the circles in half, then in half again, and once more to form pie shapes. Assure children that the folds don't need to be exact. Let children use their imaginations and muscles to tear small bits from the three sides of their pie shapes. Have children tear as many holes as they like, but make sure the holes don't touch each other. When children are finished tearing the holes, have them open the paper circles to see the beautiful, snowy designs and patterns.

Have children sit in a circle with their snowflakes, hold them in the air, and look at them. Point out that the pattern of each snowflake is different from the others just as God made each of us different. Open your Bible to Romans 12:6a, show children the passage, and read it aloud. Ask:

• **Why do you think God gave each one of us different things we do well?**

• **What's one thing you do well?**

Say: **God made each one of us special because he loves us so much.**

Lead children in this action song to the tune of "Eency Weency Spider."

One little snowflake fell from up above. *(Holding your snowflakes, pretend to let one float to the ground.)*

Then came a second flake, white just like a dove. *(Pretend to let the second snowflake float to the ground.)*

When the ground was covered *("float" the snowflakes back and forth, showing snow-covered ground),*

The children pranced with glee. *("Dance" the snowflakes back and forth.)*

Each little snowflake's special *(continue moving snowflakes),*

Just like you and me! *(Put snowflakes over your heart.)*

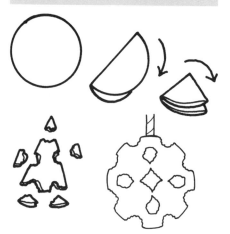

1 CORINTHIANS

"Don't you know that you yourselves are God's temple and that God's Spirit lives in you?"

1 Corinthians 3:16

1 CORINTHIANS 10:13b

THEME:
God never turns away from us.

SUMMARY:
Use this game to teach children that God is always faithful.

PREPARATION:
You'll need a Bible.

Gather children and have them stand in a tight circle, touching shoulder to shoulder. Say: **We're going to play a trusting game. I need one person to stand in the middle of our circle. That person will slowly fall forward or backward, and we'll catch him or her. When you catch someone, gently push the person back toward the middle of the circle.**

Choose a volunteer and have the child stand in the center of the circle with arms at his or her side and feet together. Have the child slowly sway backward or forward and guide others in catching the child. After about thirty seconds, let another child be in the middle. Continue the game until each child has had a turn. Then have children sit in a circle, and ask:

• **What was it like to be in the middle of the circle?**

• **What would have happened if we all turned away from the person in the middle?**

Open your Bible to 1 Corinthians 10:13b, show children the passage, and read it aloud. Say: **This means that God never turns away from us. When we're afraid or scared or sad, God will help us. He will always catch us and help us, just like we helped each other in our game.** Lead children in singing this song to the tune of "Are You Sleeping?" as a reminder of God's faithfulness.

God is faithful.
God is faithful.
All the time.
All the time.
God won't let us fall—
Not one bit at all!
We can trust.
We can trust.

1 CORINTHIANS 12:17

THEME:
We are special to God.

SUMMARY:
Use this craft to teach children we each have a special job in God's family.

PREPARATION:

You'll need a Bible; five different extracts such as vanilla, almond, peppermint, cinnamon, and lemon; and five containers. For each child you'll also need five large marshmallows, five craft sticks, and a twelve-inch length of ribbon.

Before the activity, pour each extract into separate containers. Place five marshmallows and five craft sticks at each workplace. Do this ahead of time so the marshmallows will dry out a little.

Have children sit in a circle on the floor. Open your Bible to 1 Corinthians 12:17, show children the passage, and read it aloud. Say: **The Bible teaches us that every part of our body is important.** Have children close their eyes, and ask:

• **What can you see without your eyes?**

Have children sit on their hands, and ask:

• **What can you pick up without your hands?**

Have children pinch their noses shut, and ask:

• **What can you smell?**

• **Can your ears or eyes smell?**

• **Can your hands hear?**

Say: **We need every part of our body to do its own job, just as we need every one of us to do our own job as part of God's family. We're going to make special-smelling marshmallow bouquets to remind us that when we work together, we make a beautiful-smelling bouquet for God.**

Have children move to the art area. Have children each insert one craft stick into each of their five marshmallows. Then show children how to quickly dip their marshmallows into the different extracts and wipe the excess on the edge of the container so the marshmallows don't get soggy. After children each have made five different "flowers," help them tie the flower "stems" together with a ribbon.

1 CORINTHIANS 13:4

THEME:

Love is not envious.

SUMMARY:

Use this devotion to teach children that God doesn't want us to be envious of others.

PREPARATION:

You'll need a Bible, a shallow pan of lime-flavored gelatin, table knives, and napkins.

Before this activity, prepare the gelatin according to the "Jigglers" recipe on the package.

Open your Bible to 1 Corinthians 13:4, show children the passage, and read it aloud. Teach children this verse and the motions.

Love *(hug yourself)*

Is kind *(draw a smile on your face with both pointer fingers)*,

And is not *(shake your head "no")*

Envious. *(Make a frown on your face.)*

Ask:

• **What do you think it means to be envious?**

Say: **When we're envious of others, we want what they have. And when we want what others**

have, **we're not thankful for what God has given us.**

Ask:

• **What are you thankful for?**

Say: **We're going to have a special snack to help us remember not to envy others.**

Help children each cut a large crescent shape out of the gelatin. Have them each hold their crescent shape like a frown as you say: **God doesn't want us to be envious. It makes God sad when we envy others.**

Then have kids each hold their crescent shape like a smile. Say: **God wants us to be happy when others are happy. It makes God happy when we don't envy others. Let's gobble up any envy we may have.**

Have children eat their snacks. Close with the following prayer:

Thank you, God, for all our blessings.

Take envy away and make us happy for others.

Amen.

1 CORINTHIANS 14:15

THEME:

God wants us to spend time with him.

SUMMARY:

Use this field trip to teach children that any time is the right time to spend time with God.

PREPARATION:

You'll need picnic food items, paper products, a blanket, and a Bible.

Tell children you're taking them on a surprise adventure. Have children form a line and escort them around your church to a designated picnic spot in the yard. Have children help you spread out the blanket and set out the picnic feast.

Lead children in the following prayer:

Thank you, God, for this food to eat.

Thank you for our picnic treat. Thank you for our time with you.

Thank you, God, for all you do. Amen.

As you eat your picnic, say: **It's fun to have planned activities like** birthday parties, and to do things without planning beforehand, like our picnic.

Ask:

• **What do you like best about unplanned activities?**

• **What do you like best about planned activities?**

• **Do we need planned or un-planned time to show God that we love him? Why?**

• **What are some ways we can show God how much we love him?**

Open your Bible to 1 Corinthians 14:15, show children the passage, and read it aloud. Say: **It makes God happy any time we spend time with him. Sometimes we plan time with God, such as when we pray before we eat or when we go to church. But we can also tell God we love him any time. Time we spend with God is special because we love him and he loves us.**

After your picnic, have children help clean up the picnic area, and return to the classroom.

1 CORINTHIANS 15:58

THEME:

We can give good gifts to God.

SUMMARY:

Use this devotion to teach children that God is pleased when we do good deeds.

PREPARATION:

You'll need a Bible, crayons, and a box wrapped in plain white paper.

Have kids sit in a circle. Place the gift box and crayons in the center of the circle. Ask:

• **What is the best present you've ever received?**

• **What kind of presents would you give God?**

Say: **Let's pretend this box is a present we're giving to God. We're going to give God a special present by giving him our love. To show that we're giving ourselves to God, we'll pass around the box and let each person put his or her hand print on the paper. Then tell something that you can do to show your love for God.**

Begin by outlining the shape of your hand on the box, and then tell something you can do to show how much you love God. Pass the box around the circle and let children add their hand prints while they share.

When everyone has added a hand print, open your Bible to 1 Corinthians 15:58, show children the passage, and read it aloud. Say: **This means that we are to do everything as if we are doing it for God. That means that all our actions can be like gifts to God. Let's say a prayer as our special gift to God.**

Lead children in the following prayer:

God, I give you my voice as I shout and sing. *(Hold hands to mouth.)*

I'll praise and thank my God and King! *(Raise hands.)*

I give you my hands when I serve and hug. *(Clap hands, then hug self.)*

I want everyone to know your love. *(Open arms wide.)*

God, I give you my feet. Please help me, though *(stomp feet)*,

To run and walk where you want me to go. *(Walk in place.)*

Most of all, God, I give you my heart. *(Cross hands over heart.)*

Take all that I am and not just one part. *(Open arms wide.)*

Amen.

2 CORINTHIANS

"Therefore, if anyone is in Christ, he is a new creation; the old has gone, the new has come!"

2 Corinthians 5:17

2 CORINTHIANS 2:14

THEME:

God wants us to share Jesus' love with others.

SUMMARY:

Use this object lesson to teach children that knowing Jesus is like a sweet fragrance.

PREPARATION:

You'll need a Bible, cornstarch, a tablespoon, scented bath oil or essential oil (found at a specialty shop), food coloring, a baby food jar with a lid, a three-inch square of netting, and a rubber band.

Before the activity, put two tablespoons of cornstarch in a baby food jar. Add several drops of oil and one drop of food coloring to the jar. Put on the lid and shake the jar until all the contents are blended. Remove the lid and cover the jar mouth with the netting. Put a rubber band around the jar neck to hold the netting in place. Replace the lid tightly on the jar.

Open your Bible to 2 Corinthians 2:14, show children the passage, and read it aloud. Say: **This means that knowing Jesus is like** a sweet smell or a fragrance. We can keep what we know about Jesus tightly shut up in ourselves, or we can share Jesus' love with others.

Pass around the jar and have children try to smell the scent with the lid on. Ask:

• **What does this smell like to you?**

Say: **We can't smell the fragrance when it's shut up tight in the jar.** Shake the jar, remove the lid, and pass it around for the children to smell. Ask:

• **Now what do you smell?**

• **Why do you think we could smell the fragrance this time?**

Say: **We couldn't smell the fragrance when it was closed up tight inside the jar. If we keep Jesus closed up inside our hearts, we can't share his love with others.**

Lead children in this prayer.

Help us, God, to share Jesus' love

With people that we meet,

To open our hearts and share with others,

His fragrance, oh so sweet.

Amen.

2 CORINTHIANS 3:18

THEME:

We are transformed by God.

SUMMARY:

Use this object lesson to teach children that God changes us to be more like Jesus.

PREPARATION:

You'll need a Bible, a bar magnet, a nail, and paper clips. Due to the varying power of individual magnets, try this ahead of time to determine exactly how long the nail needs to be exposed to the magnet.

Have children sit in a circle on the floor. Let children each have a turn using the magnet to pick up the nail and a paper clip. Ask:

• **What do you think magnets are used for?**

Have children each try to pick up a paper clip with the nail. Ask:

• **Why do you think you couldn't pick up the paper clip with the nail?**

Say: **This nail and the paper clips are both made out of metals that cling to magnets, but the metals don't cling to each other.**

For the metals to cling together, one of them has to be changed.

Rub the nail in one direction over the bar magnet about forty times. Then pick up a paper clip with the nail. Ask:

• **How did that happen?**

Say: **The nail was transformed. That means it was changed. By rubbing the nail across the magnet, it changed the nail.**

Open your Bible to 2 Corinthians 3:18, show children the passage, and read it aloud. Say: **This passage means that God changes us to be more like him. Just like the nail changed when it touched the magnet, we're changed by Jesus when he touches our lives.**

Ask:

• **In what ways would you like to be more like Jesus?**

Lead children in the following rhyming prayer:

Change us, Jesus, to be more like you,

In everything we say and do. Amen.

2 CORINTHIANS 5:17

THEME:

Jesus makes us new.

SUMMARY:

Use this devotion idea to teach children that when we believe in Jesus, we are made new.

PREPARATION:

You'll need a Bible, yellow construction paper, tape, scissors, markers, and two pennies for each butterfly.

Before the activity, cut out butterflies from construction paper. You'll need one butterfly for you and one for each child. Using markers, decorate one butterfly. Then tape a penny ¼-inch from the edge of each lower wing tip. Set the other butterfly cutouts, pennies, and markers on the craft table.

Have children sit in a circle away from the craft area. Have a helper hold out his or her index finger while you balance the center of your butterfly on the tip of the child's finger.

Say: **This butterfly reminds me of what happens in our lives** when we trust Jesus. Once, the butterfly was just a creeping little caterpillar on the ground, but as it followed God's plan, it climbed up under a leaf, spun a cocoon, and became a butterfly. As God worked his plan, that little creeping creature became a beautiful butterfly, like this one who's perched on our helper's finger. If God could make such a big change in a little caterpillar, imagine what he can do for you and me when we trust him and follow his plans for us.

Open your Bible to 2 Corinthians 5:17, show children the passage, and read it aloud. Say: **That means that when you belong to Jesus, you are made new.**

Ask:

• **What do you think it means to be made new?**

• **What are some ways Jesus has changed you?**

Have children move to the craft table. Give each child a butterfly cutout and have him or her decorate it with the markers. Help children tape pennies to the bottom wings of their butterflies. When finished, have children balance their butterflies on their fingers as you lead them in the following paraphrase of the Scripture verse:

In Jesus, I am made new.
The old is gone.
Everything is new.

2 CORINTHIANS 8:7

THEME:

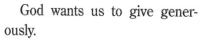

God wants us to give generously.

SUMMARY:

Use this service idea to teach children that we can show God's love by helping others.

PREPARATION:

You'll need a Bible, large cardboard boxes, butcher paper to cover the boxes, tape, markers, address labels, a CD player, a CD of lively praise music, and a cardboard tube.

Enlist the help of everyone who can help you publicize this drive. Put notices in your church newsletter and bulletin asking for donations of coloring books and crayons.

Arrange for a place to donate the items you'll collect, such as a pediatrician's office, a public health clinic, or a local social service agency—anywhere children have to wait.

Before the activity, tape butcher paper over the outside of the boxes. Prepare a label for each donated item. Write something such as, "Placed by the preschoolers at [name of your church] to help make your wait more enjoyable."

Gather children together and say: **We're going to play a game called Freeze and Wait. I'll turn on the music, and you'll be able to move in different ways all over the room. When the music stops, you must freeze. Then I'll turn the music back on, but you can't start moving again until I touch you with my thawing wand.** Show them the cardboard tube. Say: **I have to warn you, though, I can hardly move when I get cold!**

Turn on the music, and let the fun begin. Stop the music and wait for everyone to freeze. When everyone is still, remind them that they can't move until you've touched them with the wand. Turn the music back on and say: **It's so cold in here, I can hardly move!**

Begin moving toward the children in slow motion, and touch each one. Then stop the music again and repeat the whole process several times. The last time, let them move freely a bit longer, then stop the music and ask the children to be seated where they are. Ask:

• **What was the hardest part of this game?**

• **How do you feel about waiting?**

• **What do you do while you're waiting?**

Say: **Waiting is one of the hardest things for preschoolers to do. It really helps if you have something to do while you're waiting. One of the places in our town that children most often have to wait is** [tell the kids where you will place your collected items].

Open your Bible to 2 Corinthians 8:7, show children the passage, and read it aloud. Say: **This passage tells us to be generous in showing love to others and in giving to others. One way we can help show God's love is by helping children do something that's really hard for them, like waiting. I've noticed that one of the things that helps preschoolers wait is coloring. We're going to give coloring books and crayons to help preschoolers at** [name of place] **while they wait.**

Explain to children that you're asking families in your church to bring crayons and coloring books to give to children while they wait.

Have children work in teams to color and decorate the collection boxes with markers. Hang a sign on each box to tell people what the boxes are for. Then take the preschoolers to place the boxes in strategic areas of the church. When you return to the classroom, say: **It will be fun over the next couple of weeks to watch the crayons and coloring books come in. Each week, we'll empty the boxes and put special labels on the coloring books and crayons. Then we'll place them aside until it's time to deliver them.**

As the children work, help them sing this song to the tune of "Mary Had a Little Lamb."

> **We all want to show God's love,**
>   **Show God's love,**
>   **Show God's love.**
>   **We all want to show God's love**
>   **In everything we do.**

After a few weeks, donate the items to the place(s) with whom you made arrangements.

2 CORINTHIANS 9:7

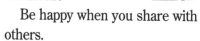

THEME:

Be happy when you share with others.

SUMMARY:

Use this song to teach children that God loves a cheerful giver.

PREPARATION:

You'll need a Bible.

Open your Bible to 2 Corinthians 9:7, show children the passage, and read it aloud. Say: **This passage means that God wants us to be cheerful and happy when we give to others. He doesn't want us to be fussy or angry when we share.**

Ask:

• **Why does God want us to be happy when we give to others?**

• **How do you think God feels when we fuss or get angry about** sharing?

• **How can we show others that we're cheerful givers?**

Say: **When we're cheerful givers, we show God that we love him.**

Lead children in the following song and motions to the tune of "If You're Happy and You Know It."

If you're happy when you share, show a smile. *(Smile big, and point to your face, making a wide grin with your fingers.)*

If you're happy when you share, show a smile. *(Smile big, and point to your face, making a wide grin with your fingers.)*

If you're happy when you share *(smile big, and point to your face, making a wide grin with your fingers),*

You show God you really care. *(Point up, and nod "yes.")*

If you're happy when you share, show a smile. *(Smile big, and point to your face, making a wide grin with your fingers.)*

GALATIANS

"You are all sons of God through faith in Christ Jesus."

Galatians 3:26

GALATIANS 5:22-23

THEME:

God gives us fruits of the Spirit.

SUMMARY:

Use this music idea to teach children that God gives us good things.

PREPARATION:

You'll need a Bible, apples, bananas, and oranges.

Before the activity, cut up the apples, bananas, and oranges into bite-size pieces. Save one whole apple, banana, and orange for circle time.

Have children sit in a circle. Place the whole fruits in the middle of the circle. Help children name the different kinds of fruits.

Say: **God has given us good fruits to eat. He has also given us special fruits to carry inside us. Let's find out what they are.**

Open your Bible to Galatians 5:22-23, show children the passage, and read it aloud. Say: **This passage tells us that the Holy Spirit gives us love, joy, kindness, peace, and other special fruits that show in the way we act.**

Ask:
• **How can we show love? joy? kindness?**
• **How does God feel when we act this way? Why?**

Say: **Let's learn a song to remind us of the special fruits that God gives us.** Lead children in singing this song to the tune of "Here We Go 'Round the Mulberry Bush."

> **The fruits of the Spirit are love, joy, peace,**
>   **Love, joy, peace,**
>   **Love, joy, peace.**
> **The fruits of the Spirit are love, joy, peace,**
>   **All through the day.**

After singing the song, lead children in prayer, thanking God for the fruits of the Spirit, and for giving us good fruits to eat. Serve the prepared fruit pieces to children for a snack.

GALATIANS 6:9

THEME:

Do not grow weary.

SUMMARY:

Use this object lesson to teach children that we will reap a harvest if we don't give up.

PREPARATION:

You'll need a Bible, heavy whipping cream, plastic knives, bread or crackers, and one baby food jar with its lid for every six children.

Pour about one inch of cream into each jar and tightly screw on the lid.

Have children sit in a circle on the floor. Ask:

• What's one way to make a friend?

Say: **Being kind is a good way to make a friend.**

Ask:

• Is one act of kindness enough to make and keep a friendship?

Form groups of six. Give each group a jar of cream, and have the children shake the jar and pass it around their circle. When the children receive the jar, have them say one way to be kind to a friend, then pass it on to the next person. Continue around the circle until the cream changes to butter. Then collect the jars. Ask:

• Was it easy to make butter?

• Is it always easy to be kind? Why or why not?

Open your Bible to Galatians 6:9, show children the passage, and read it aloud. Say: **This passage tells us not to grow tired and weary when we do good things.**

Ask:

• Why does God want us to do good things?

• How can we be good to our friends?

Drain the liquid from the butter and spread the butter on bread or crackers so children can taste the harvest of their labor.

EPHESIANS

"For it is by grace you have been saved,
through faith—and this not from yourselves,
it is the gift of God."

Ephesians 2:8

EPHESIANS 4:32

THEME:

Be kind to other people.

SUMMARY:

Use this song to teach children that Jesus wants us to be kind to one another.

PREPARATION:

You'll need a Bible.

Gather children together. Open your Bible to Ephesians 4:32, and read it aloud. Say: **It makes God happy when we're kind to others.**

Ask:

• **Why do you think God wants us to be kind to others?**

• **In what ways can we be kind to others?**

Say: **Let's learn a song to help us remember that God wants us to be kind to others.** Lead children in singing this song to the tune of "She'll Be Coming 'Round the Mountain." Let children dance around the room as they sing.

We'll be kind to one another. Yes, we will!
We'll be kind to one an-

other. Yes, we will!
We'll be kind to one another—
To our sisters and our brothers.
We'll be kind to one another. Yes, we will!

We'll be kind to one another. Yes, we will!
We'll be kind to one another. Yes, we will!
We'll be kind to one another—
To our fathers and our mothers.
We'll be kind to one another. Yes, we will!

We'll be kind to one another. Yes, we will!
We'll be kind to one another. Yes, we will!
We'll be kind to one another—
Learn to love and help each other.
We'll be kind to one another. Yes, we will!

EPHESIANS 5:8-9

THEME:

Let your light for Jesus shine through.

SUMMARY:

Use this affirmation activity to teach children that they are light to the world.

PREPARATION:

You'll need a Bible and a flashlight.

Have children sit in a circle. Turn off the lights, and pull out a flashlight. Open your Bible to Ephesians 5:8-9, show children the passage using the flashlight, and read it aloud. Say: **God made us children of light. We each have special things about us that help us shine.**

Ask:

• **How do you feel knowing that you are special to God?**

Choose a "Spotlight Person." Shine the light on a child in your group and ask that child to tell three things about him- or herself, such as family members' names, favorite things to do, and a special talent. Have the group clap for that child and say: **You shine for Jesus.** Repeat this for each child.

Ask:

• **How can you share your special talents with others?**

• **How does God feel when we use the gifts he has given us?**

Close in prayer, thanking God that we are special to him, and ask him to help us shine our light to others.

EPHESIANS 6:16

THEME:

God is always with us.

SUMMARY:

Use this craft idea to teach children that God is our protection.

PREPARATION:

You'll need a Bible, paper grocery sacks, scissors, paint-stirring sticks (available for free at most paint and hardware stores), transparent tape, crayons, aluminum foil, and old newspaper.

Before the activity, cut the bottoms from paper grocery sacks, then cut the sacks vertically in half. Cut one paper-sack "shield" for each child. Set out crayons, transparent tape, and small pieces of aluminum foil.

Open your Bible to Ephesians 6:16, show children the passage, and read it aloud. Say: **Shields were used in battle to protect warriors. This passage tells us that we can use the shield of faith to protect us. Knowing that God is with us is our shield of faith. He protects us.**

Ask:

• **How do you feel knowing that God is always with you? Why?**

Say: **Today we're going to make shields to remind us that God protects us.**

Give each child a paper shield. Have children use crayons to decorate their shields then tape bits of shiny foil to the shields to make them really shine!

Help each child securely tape a paint stick across the back of his or her shield. Place tape only at the ends of the paint-stirring sticks so children can slide their hands around the center of the sticks to hold their shields.

After children have finished their shields, play this action game. Hand each child a half-sheet of newspaper to crumple. When you say "go," have kids toss the paper wads at each other and hold up the shields to deflect the flying paper. Toss the paper "arrows" again and again for a few minutes, then ask children to toss their arrows in the wastebasket. Close in prayer, thanking God that he protects us.

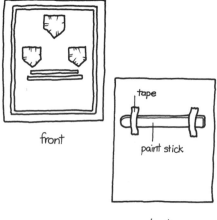

front

tape

paint stick

back

PHILIPPIANS

"Rejoice in the Lord always. I will say it again: Rejoice!"

Philippians 4:4

PHILIPPIANS 2:19-23

THEME:

God wants us to be good friends.

SUMMARY:

Use this game to teach children about Timothy helping Paul.

PREPARATION:

You'll need a Bible and blindfolds.

Form pairs and give them each a blindfold. Designate a base. Choose one pair to be "It." Have one partner of each pair put the blindfold over his or her eyes. Have partners hold hands and stand by the wall opposite the base. Have partners get to the base without being tagged by "It." If either partner is tagged, that pair becomes "It" also and tries to tag other pairs.

Play until everyone is either caught or on the base. Have partners switch roles and play again. Ask:

• **How did you help your partner in this game? How do friends help each other?**

Open your Bible to Philippians 2:19-23, show children the passage, and paraphrase the passage. Ask:

• **What kinds of things do you do to help your friends?**

• **What kinds of things do you think Timothy did to help his friend Paul?**

• **How do you help friends when they're sad?**

• **How can you help a friend this week?**

Say: **You can be like Timothy and do nice things for your friends when they need help.**

Close in prayer, asking God to help us be good friends like Timothy.

PHILIPPIANS 4:14, 16

THEME:

God wants us to help those in need.

SUMMARY:

Use this service project to teach children about helping others.

PREPARATION:

You'll need a Bible, a cot, blanket, pillow, small bedside table, vase of silk flowers, food tray, plate, cup, napkin, a place setting of silverware, blocks of green floral foam, small (two to three inches long) baskets, small silk flowers, plain paper, and colored markers.

Before the activity, cut the floral foam to fit into the baskets. Call a local community-service program that takes meals to shut-ins, or to a local hospital's dietary department to gain permission to place the favors on their meal trays. Make plans to deliver the table favors.

Set up a make-believe hospital area in your classroom by setting out a cot with a blanket and a pillow; a bedside table with flowers on it; and a tray with a plate, a cup, a napkin, and silverware on it.

As children arrive, give them an opportunity to play in the hospital setting for several minutes. Then gather the children together. Ask:

• **Have you ever been in a real hospital? What was it like?**

• **Has your mom or dad ever brought you a meal in bed when you were sick at home? What was that like?**

• **How does it feel to be sick and unable to do the things you like to do?**

Say: **It's not fun to be sick and have to stay in bed all the time. There are people in our church and in our community who are too sick to get out of bed, go outside, or fix their own meals. In the Bible, Paul sent a thank-you letter to some people who helped him.**

Open your Bible to Philippians 4:14, 16, show children the passage, and read it aloud. Say: **Just like Paul had help, God wants us to help people who need us while they're sick. We're going to send aid to these people by making some special decorations to put on the trays of the people who have their meals delivered to them.**

Set out small baskets, small silk flowers, and green floral foam in one area of your classroom, and set out paper and colored markers in another area. Half the class will make place mats by drawing pictures on the paper. The other half of the students will place the flowers in the baskets by sticking the stems in the green floral foam. After each group has finished, have kids trade places so each student has an opportunity to make a flower basket and draw a place mat.

COLOSSIANS

*"Do all these things; but most important,
love each other. Love is what holds you all
together in perfect unity."*

Colossians 3:14, New Century Version

COLOSSIANS 1:16

THEME:

God wants us to enjoy all the great things he made.

SUMMARY:

Use this devotion to teach children that God wants us to enjoy all the great things he made.

PREPARATION:

You'll need a Bible and enough animal cookies for each child to have at least one.

Gather children together and say: **God made all different kinds of animals for us to enjoy. Let's play a game about God's different animals. Each one of you will get a turn choosing an animal cookie. When you choose a cookie, tell us what animal it is, and we'll act out that animal. Then you can eat your cookie. I'm hungry as a horse, so let's get started!**

Begin the game by giving each child a turn to choose a cookie. One at a time, have children tell what animal they picked, and have everyone act out the animal's noise and an action that animal would make. If some children pick an animal that has al-ready been acted out, have children act out that animal again. When everyone has had a turn, ask:

• **What are some other animals that God created?**

• **What are some other things besides animals that God created?**

Say: **The Bible tells us that everything was made by God.** Show children Colossians 1:16 in the Bible, and read it aloud.

God created everything that we see. Even when you see people building a house, you can remember that God made the wood, the sand that makes bricks, the material that makes glass windows, even the metal nails come from rocks that God created. God is creative and he wants us to enjoy all the great things he made.

Close in prayer, thanking God for all his creation.

COLOSSIANS 3:12

THEME:

God wants us to care for others.

SUMMARY:

Use this field trip to teach children about how missionaries show God's love to others, and make a banner to send to missionaries.

PREPARATION:

You'll need a Bible, a globe or map, crayons, and a sheet of banner paper with the words "Thank you for being our missionaries!" written in the center.

Before the activity, arrange to take your preschoolers to visit your pastor or the teacher of another class.

Say: Today we're going to learn about missionaries.

Ask:

• Who knows what a missionary is?

• What does a missionary do?

Say: **A missionary is a person who travels, or goes on a mission, to tell others about Jesus. A mission is a journey with an important purpose. Let's pretend we're missionaries right now and go on**

a mission trip to tell others what we know about Jesus. But first let's think about what we will say.

Ask:

• **What do you know about Jesus?**

Say: **Those are good things we can tell others about Jesus. Now let's go on our mission.**

Lead children to another room in the church for your prearranged visit with your pastor or a teacher. Have children share the things they know about Jesus. Return to your classroom and say: **That was quite a trip! You did a wonderful job telling about Jesus. Let's imagine what that trip might have been like if we were real missionaries and we had to travel far from home.**

Ask:

• **How would you feel if you were far from home?**

• **What do you think it would be like if the people we visited didn't speak our language?**

Say: **Missionaries from many churches are busy telling others about Jesus.**

Point on the globe to the area where church's missionaries are active. Ask:

• **What kind of food do you think they eat there?**

• **What do you think the weather is like there?**

Give children a summary of what life is like in that part of the world, and tell them about a missionary family who lives there.

Say: **Missionaries go to a lot of trouble to tell others about Jesus. They might have to go far from home. They might have to eat strange food. They might get homesick or lonely. But we can help! We can let them know we care about them. Listen to what the Bible says about caring for others.** Open your Bible to Colossians 3:12, show children the passage, and read it aloud.

Say: **Let's show a missionary family how much we care about them by sending a banner.**

Have children draw pictures and help them sign their names on the banner. Send the banner to a missionary family from your church or denomination.

1 THESSALONIANS

"May the Lord make your love increase and overflow for each other and for everyone else, just as ours does for you."

1 Thessalonians 3:12

1 THESSALONIANS 1:4

THEME:

We are chosen by God.

SUMMARY:

Use this quiet reflection to teach children that God has chosen us as his children because he loves us.

PREPARATION:

You'll need a Bible.

Have children sit in a circle. Say: **I need some helpers. I wonder who I can choose to help me.** [Child's name], **I need you to help me.**

Continue slowly calling each child's name to be your helper until you've called all the children's names. Ask:

• **How did you feel when I chose you as a helper? Why?**

• **Can you think of a time when you weren't chosen for something?**

• **How did that feel? Why?**

Say: **It makes us feel special when we're chosen.**

Open your Bible to 1 Thessalonians 1:4, show children the passage, and read it aloud. Say: **This passage** tells us that God loves us and has chosen us to be his.

Ask:

• **How do you feel knowing that God chose you because he loves you? Why?**

Say: **I need all my helpers to help me say this prayer of thanksgiving to God.**

Have children repeat each verse after you:

Thank you, God,
For choosing me.
Thank you, God,
For loving me.
Thank you, God,
That I am special to you.
Amen.

1 THESSALONIANS 5:21

THEME:

God wants us to test all things.

SUMMARY:

Use this object lesson to teach children that God doesn't want us to be fooled by things that are bad.

PREPARATION:

You'll need a Bible and equal amounts of the following pairs of items: granulated sugar and table salt, hot cocoa mix and powdered cocoa, and iced tea and cider vinegar.

Before the activity, set out the items in pairs together on a table.

Gather children around the table and say: **I've set out two kinds of sugar, hot cocoa mix, and iced tea. One kind is real and one is an impostor. An impostor is something that looks real but isn't the same. It's a phony or a fake.**

Ask:

• **How can we tell which is real and which is an impostor?**

Have kids explore by tasting, smelling, or touching the items in each group. Ask:

• **Which of the things in these pairs taste good?**

• **Which taste bad?**

Say: **Sometimes it's difficult to tell the real from the phony or the good from the bad.** Open the Bible to 1 Thessalonians 5:21, show children the passage, and read it aloud. **God gives us this instruction so we won't be fooled by bad things in life that look like good things.**

Ask:

• **Why doesn't God want us to be fooled by bad things?**

• **What should we do with the things we find that are bad?**

Close in prayer, asking God to help us not to be fooled by bad things.

2 THESSALONIANS

"May our Lord Jesus Christ himself and God our Father, who loved us and by his grace gave us eternal encouragement and good hope, encourage your hearts and strengthen you in every good deed and word."

2 Thessalonians 2:16-17

2 THESSALONIANS 2:13

THEME:
We are set apart for God.

SUMMARY:
Use this game to teach children that God set us apart for special things.

PREPARATION:
You'll need a Bible.

Have children stand in a line. Stand as far away from the line as you can. Then say: **I'm going to call out categories such as "wearing red" or "five years old" or "has brown hair." Every time I call out a category that describes you, you are set apart. If you fit the category, take two giant steps forward. If you don't fit the category, stay where you are, and crouch down on the floor. When** you reach me, tag me and shout, "Set apart."

Play several times with these categories: clothing colors; clothing styles such as jeans, shorts, or dresses; ages; and food preferences, such as pizza or ice cream.

After the game, gather children in a circle. Open the Bible to 2 Thessalonians 2:13, show children the passage, and read it aloud. Say: **This means that when we accept Jesus into our hearts, we are set apart for God. He has chosen us to be his children.**

When we become part of God's family, he sets us apart to do very special things. When we played our game, you were set apart when you tagged me.

Ask:

• **How is that like being set apart for God?**

• **Why does God set us apart?**

Close in prayer, thanking God for accepting us as his children and setting us apart for special things.

1 TIMOTHY

*"Don't let anyone look down on you because
you are young, but set an example
for the believers in speech, in life,
in love, in faith and in purity."*

1 Timothy 4:12

1 TIMOTHY 1:14

THEME:

God pours out his grace on us.

SUMMARY:

Use this object lesson to teach children the concept of grace.

PREPARATION:

You'll need a Bible, a box of round crackers, paper lunch sacks, and a sign made from poster board that says "Bank."

Gather children together and ask:

• **Who has a piggy bank?**

• **What do you do with your piggy bank?**

Say: **Adults use a different kind of bank. At a bank, they hold your money for safekeeping until you need it.**

• **Have you ever been to a bank before?**

• **What was it like?**

Say: **We're going to make a pretend trip to a bank.** Hand each child a paper lunch sack, and tell children that the sacks are their "money bags" where they'll put their money.

Place the "Bank" sign and several stacks of crackers on a table. Say:

This is a pretend bank with stacks of make-believe money. I'll be the banker. I'll call you to the bank, and then I'll give you each one "coin" for your money bag. Don't let anyone peek into your money bag after your trip to the bank.

Call each child to the bank, but instead of one cracker coin, give each child a small handful of coins.

After everyone has gone to the bank, ask:

• **How did you feel when you got a lot of coins instead of just one?**

• **Why do you think you got more than you expected?**

As children munch their crunchy coins, say: **You only expected one coin, but instead, you got many coins. And you didn't have to work for those coins or earn them. That's the way God's grace works. God gives us his grace and love as free gifts, and he always gives us more than we can imagine. Let's see what the Bible says about God's grace.**

Open your Bible to 1 Timothy 1:14, show children the passage, and read it aloud. Say: **When God pours out his grace on us, we're filled with his love. We don't have to pay a thing for God's grace. God's grace is a free gift that he gives us because he loves us so much.**

Close with this prayer:

Dear God, thank you for the free gift of your grace. Thank you for filling us to overflowing with your love. We love you. Amen.

1 TIMOTHY 2:1

THEME:
We can pray for others.

SUMMARY:
Use this prayer activity to teach children that they can intercede for others with prayer.

PREPARATION:
You'll need a Bible.

Gather children and ask:
• **What is prayer?**
• **What things do you pray for?**
Say: **God always hears our prayers, and he answers them in his time and in his own way. Many prayers we pray are for ourselves, but did you know that we're supposed to pray for others, too? Let's find out what the Bible says about praying for others.**

Open the Bible to 1 Timothy 2:1, show children the passage, and read it aloud. Ask:
• **Why does God want us to pray for others?**
Say: **When we pray for others, we ask God for things they need, or we ask God to help care for those people. Let's learn a prayer that we can sing when we pray for others.**

Teach children this song to the tune of "Jesus Loves Me."

Whether I'm at home or play,
God is with me every day.
Thank you, God, for being near.
When I pray, I know you hear.

I pray for [name].
I pray for [name].
I pray for [name].
God watch over them today.

Lead children in singing the song. When you get to the lines "I pray for [name]," go around the circle and let children each insert the name of someone they want to pray for. Repeat the song until each child has had a turn to pray.

2 TIMOTHY

*"You then, my son, be strong in the grace
that is in Christ Jesus."*

2 Timothy 2:1

2 TIMOTHY 3:16-17

THEME:

The Bible is our instruction book.

SUMMARY:

Use this devotion idea to teach children that the Bible is full of stories to teach us.

PREPARATION:

You'll need a Bible and several boxes of graduated sizes that will fit inside one another.

Before the activity, place a Bible inside the smallest box, place the boxes inside one another, and gift-wrap the largest box.

Have children sit in a circle. Ask:
• **What do you think is in my box?**

Pass the box around the circle and let children shake and rattle the box. After children have each had a turn to guess, let them help you unwrap the first box. Open the box and reveal the next box. Show children the box, then shake and rattle it. Continue opening each box until you open the smallest box to reveal the Bible. Say: **It's a Bible.**

Ask:

• **What do you think we'll find in here?**

Say: **The Bible is God's Word—a collection of many different stories. In fact, the Bible is like a library! The Bible is also a lot like my big box. When we opened it, we found smaller boxes inside. If we open the Bible, we find lots of smaller books, chapters, and stories inside.**

Open your Bible and show children the table of contents, the Old Testament and the New Testament sections, and some of the books.

Say: **All of the stories in the Bible come from God. I'm not sure just how many stories are actually in this Bible, but I do know that they are all given to us by God so that we can learn from them.**

Open your Bible to 2 Timothy 3:16-17, show children the passage, and read it aloud. Say: **This tells us that the Bible contains all the information we need to know how God wants us to live. The Bible is our instruction book.**

Close with a song of prayer.

Say: **Let's sing "The B-I-B-L-E." When we sing the word "stand," I want all of you to stand up.**

Sing this song twice with the children.

**The B-I-B-L-E,
Yes, that's the book for me.**

I stand alone on the Word of God,

The B-I-B-L-E!

Amen.

2 TIMOTHY 4:2

THEME:

We can share the good news of God's love.

SUMMARY:

Use this snack idea to teach children that it's our responsibility to tell others about God.

PREPARATION:

You'll need a Bible, jelly, peanut butter (check for allergies), several plastic knives, and crackers.

Have children sit in a circle. Say: **I want to make a peanut butter and jelly cracker, but I need you to help me. I'll do just what you say as you tell me how to make my peanut butter and jelly cracker.**

Follow the kids' instructions exactly. If they say "put the peanut butter on the cracker," set the entire jar on top of the cracker. If they tell you to open the jar and put the jelly on the cracker, turn the jar almost upside down, as if you're trying to dump the jelly out onto the cracker. Make it comical, and illustrate that kids must be clear in their instructions.

When you're finished, say: **Finally we're finished! Thank you for helping me make a peanut butter and jelly cracker. There's something else you can help others learn.**

Ask:

• **How do people know God loves them and sent Jesus to be their Savior?**

Open your Bible to 2 Timothy 4:2, show children the passage, and read it aloud. Say: **This tells us that God wants us to be ready to share his love. We need to show others how to follow God. When we tell others that God loves them and how to follow him, we have to tell them step by step, just as you told me how to fix the cracker.**

Ask:

• **What are some things that you could share about following God?**

Say: **We all can share the good news about God's love. As we pray today, I would like each of you to think of someone—at school, in your family, or from your neighborhood—that you can tell about God. Keep that name in** your head, and ask God to help you talk to that person this week.

Pray: **Dear God, thank you for loving each of us so very much. I have someone special that I want to talk to about you. I know you love this person. Help me to share just what you want me to** share. **Help me to be brave and to speak clearly with this person this week. I know you will give me the words to make your message of love shine through me. Amen.**

Help children each make one or two peanut butter and jelly crackers to eat for a snack.

TITUS

"But when the kindness and love of God our Savior appeared, he saved us, not because of righteous things we had done, but because of his mercy."

Titus 3:4-5a

PHILEMON 4

THEME:

Pray for each other.

SUMMARY:

Use this prayer idea to teach children that God wants us to say prayers of thanksgiving for one another.

PREPARATION:

You'll need a Bible.

Have children sit in a circle. Open your Bible to Philemon 4, show children the passage, and read it aloud. Say: **This passage reminds us that we are to pray and thank God for each other.**

Ask:

• **Why does God want us to pray for one another?**

• **Why should we thank God for each other?**

• **How do you feel when someone prays for you? Why?**

Say: **Let's learn a fun rhyme to help us remember to pray for each other.**

Lead children in the words and motions to this rhyme:

When I say my prayers *(fold hands in prayer)*,

I'll thank God for you. *(Raise hands up and point to each other.)*

I'm glad you are my friend. *(Place hands over heart and nod "yes.")*

Please pray for me, too. *(Fold hands in prayer.)*

Say: **Let's practice praying for one another by saying pop-up prayers of thanksgiving. When it's your turn, you're going to pop up and say "Thank you, God" for the person sitting on your right. Then you'll sit down and the next person in the circle will pop up to pray. We'll continue around the circle until everyone has had a chance to pray, then we'll all shout together, "Amen!"**

Begin the pop-up prayers, prompting children when necessary.

HEBREWS

*"Therefore, since we have a great high priest
who has gone through the heavens,
Jesus the Son of God, let us hold
firmly to the faith we profess."*

Hebrews 4:14

HEBREWS 3:13

THEME:

God wants us to encourage others.

SUMMARY:

Use this game idea to teach children that we should encourage others every day.

PREPARATION:

You'll need a Bible and a whistle.

Have children form pairs. Say: **We're going to play a game where we encourage each other by telling our partners nice things about them. For example, you might tell your partner he has a nice smile or she is kind to others. Then, every time I blow the whistle, you must find new partners and say something encouraging to them.**

Blow the whistle four separate times at about twenty-second intervals. Ask:

• **How did it feel when someone encouraged you?**

• **How did it feel when you encouraged others?**

Open your Bible to Hebrews 3:13,

show children the passage, and read it aloud. Ask:

• **Why does God want us to encourage others every day?**

• **What are some ways we can encourage others?**

Say: **God wants us to help others by encouraging them every day. Think of someone you know who you can encourage today.**

Close with the following prayer: **Dear God, help us to be people who help others by our encouragement. Amen.**

HEBREWS 4:12a

THEME:

The Bible is God's living Word.

SUMMARY:

Use this devotion to teach children that the Word of God is truth for all people.

PREPARATION:

You'll need as many different kinds of Bibles as you can gather, including Bibles in several different translations, picture Bibles, study Bibles, foreign language Bibles, and devotional Bibles.

ave children sit in a circle. Hold up one of the Bibles and have children take turns describing it.

Say: **There are many ways to describe the exact same book! Even though you each noticed different things, it's still the same book. I have a lot of other books here.**

Pass the Bibles around the circle and have children look at them. Ask:

• **How are these books different?**

• **How are they the same?**

Say: **Even though the covers, the sizes, the shapes, and even the words in these books are different, they all contain the words of God. We call all these books Bibles. The Bibles may be different, but they all tell us that God loves us, guides us, and saves us.**

Open your Bible to Hebrews 4:12a, show children the passage, and read it aloud. Say: **Even though each of these Bibles is different, they're living and active because they teach us God's words. They show us how God wants us to live.**

Ask:

• **Why do you think God gives us his Word to live by?**

Close in prayer, thanking God for giving us his living Word.

HEBREWS 11:1

THEME:
I believe in Jesus.

SUMMARY:
Use this finger play to teach children that faith is believing in what we do not see.

PREPARATION:
You'll need a Bible.

pen your Bible to Hebrews 11:1, show children the passage, and read it aloud. Say: **The Bible says that faith is believing in what we do not see.**

Teach children the words and motions to this rhyme:

Faith is believing in what we do not see. *(Cover eyes with hands.)*

I believe in Jesus *(point to the sky)*,

I feel his love for me. *(Hug self.)*

After the children have said the rhyme a few times, have them stand in a large circle and pretend to be trees, holding out their arms as if they're branches. Have one child pretend to be the wind, run to each child in the circle, and blow in front of the child to create a breeze. As the "trees" feel the breeze, have them sway the way a real tree does in the wind. Have the children take turns being the wind. Ask:

• **How did you know the wind was blowing?**

• **What happened to you when the wind blew?**

Say: **You couldn't see the wind, but you could feel it. That's how you knew to start swaying like a tree. We can't see Jesus, but we believe in him. We know he is with us because we can feel him in our hearts.**

HEBREWS 11:6

THEME:

We believe in God.

SUMMARY:

Use this object lesson to teach children that we please God by believing in him.

PREPARATION:

You'll need a Bible, a red paper heart, a cross, and a variety of natural items (such as flowers and stones) put into a paper bag. Be sure to have at least one item for each child. If you can't get items from nature, use pictures.

Open your Bible to Hebrews 11:6, show children the passage, and read it aloud. Say: **This verse means that we please God by believing in him.**

Have kids sit in a circle on the floor. Have children take turns reaching into the bag and pulling out an item. When kids remove an item from the bag, have them tell how that item can help us believe in God. For example, a heart can remind us that God loves us; a cross can remind us that God sent Jesus; and a picture of a dog can remind us that God gives us good things, such as pets, to love. Ask:

• **Why do you think these items help us believe in God?**

• **How do you think God feels when we say we believe in him?**

• **What is something you can do to show God that you believe in him?**

Say: **One thing that pleases God is when we learn special verses from the Bible. Let's practice the Scripture verse by singing a special song.**

Lead children in singing "Believing in Him" to the tune of "Skip to My Lou." As you sing, lead kids in the actions.

Please God *(point to your happy smile)*

By believing in him. *(Point up.)*

Please God *(point to your happy smile)*

By believing in him. *(Point up.)*

Please God *(point to your happy smile)*

By believing in him. *(Point up.)*

That's what the Bible tells us. *(Make a Bible using your hands.)*

HEBREWS 13:5b-6a

THEME:

God is with us.

SUMMARY:

Use this game to teach children that we don't have to be afraid because God is always with us.

PREPARATION:

You'll need a Bible, clothespins, and small squares of paper. (You may want to use a permanent marker to write "God Never Leaves Us" on each clothespin.)

Gather children, and ask:
• **How do you feel when you're alone?**

• **Who would you like to have with you when you're afraid?**

Say: **Sometimes we feel afraid or alone. This game will help us learn about someone who is always with us.**

Give each child a square of paper, and instruct children to place the papers on their shoulders Say: **Now, see if you can shake the paper off your shoulder, without using your hands.** When children have tried this, say: **That was too easy. Let's make this game a little more challenging.**

Clip a clothespin to the back of each child's clothing, close enough to children's shoulders so they can feel and see it, but not where it can be easily reached. When every child is wearing a clothespin, say: **Now, try to shake these clothespins off, without using your hands.**

Allow children to jump, hop, shake, and move about as they try to loosen the clothespins. (They'll have a great time trying!) After a minute, gather children, and ask:

• **Which was easier to lose, the paper or the clothespin? Why?**

Open your Bible to Hebrews 13:5b-6a, show children the passage, and read it aloud. Say: **The Bible**

Close in prayer, thanking God for all the good gifts he gives us.

JAMES 2:8

THEME:

Love your neighbors.

SUMMARY:

Use this music idea to teach children that God wants us to love each other.

PREPARATION:

You'll need a Bible.

Open your Bible to James 2:8, show children the passage, and read it aloud. Say: **This verse tells us that God wants us to love our neighbors just as much as we love ourselves.**

Ask:

• **Why do you think God wants us to love our neighbors as much as we love ourselves?**

• **How can we show our neighbors we love them?**

Lead children in singing this song to the tune of "London Bridge."

> **Love your neighbor as yourself, as yourself, as yourself.**

> **Love your neighbor as yourself; love your neighbor.**

As you sing this verse, have children hug each other while they sing.

> **Give your neighbor a great big hug, great big hug, great big hug.**
> **Give your neighbor a great big hug; hug your neighbor.**

As you sing this verse, have children point to someone new with each "I love you."

> **Tell your neighbor "I love you," "I love you," "I love you."**
> **Tell your neighbor "I love you"; love your neighbor.**

JAMES 5:13

THEME:

Sing praises to God.

SUMMARY:

Use this prayer idea to teach children that we should praise God when we're happy.

PREPARATION:

You'll need a Bible.

Open your Bible to James 5:13, show children the passage, and read it aloud. Say: **We know to pray to God when we're sick or afraid, but this verse tells us to praise God when we're happy.**

Ask:

• **Why should we praise God when we're happy?**

• **What are some ways we can praise God?**

• **How do you think God feels when we praise him? Why?**

Say: **Let's sing praises to God.**

Lead children in singing this song to the tune of "If You're Happy and You Know It."

> **When you're happy and you know it, praise God.**
> **Praise God!** *(Shout echo.)*
> **When you're happy and you know it, praise God.**
> **Praise God!** *(Shout echo.)*
> **When you're happy and you know it,**
> **Praise God to really show it.**
> **When you're happy and you know it, praise God.**
> **Amen!** *(Shout.)*

JAMES 5:16

THEME:

God wants us to confess our sins.

SUMMARY:

Use this object lesson to teach children that God wants us to cleanse our hearts from sin.

PREPARATION:

You'll need a Bible, pretzels, a clear plastic bottle filled halfway with water, a clear pitcher of clean water, and paper cups.

Before this activity, add several spoonfuls of dirt to the bottle of water.

Have children sit in a circle and give each child a handful of pretzels. Munch a few pretzels yourself. Say: **I love pretzels, but they make me really thirsty! I'll bet you're thirsty too. Fortunately, I brought a bottle of cold, refreshing water!**

Hold up the bottle of dirty water. Ask:

• **Would you like a drink? Why or why not?**

Say: **Oh, that little bit of dirt won't hurt! I'll just add some** clean water and that'll make everything OK.

Pour a little clean water into the dirty bottle. Ask:

• **Did that help?**

• **What will we have to do before we can drink from this water bottle?**

Say: **Our hearts can sometimes be like this water bottle. When we sin or do bad things, our hearts get dirty.**

Ask:

• **What does it feel like when your heart is filled with bad things?**

• **What can you do when your heart gets dirty with sin?**

Open your Bible to James 5:16, show children the passage, and read it aloud. Say: **It's important to tell God about our sins and clean the "dirt" from our hearts. God wants us each to have a pure heart that'll love and serve him!**

Lead children in the following prayer:

Dear God, help us confess our sins and clean the dirt from our hearts. Give us pure hearts that love and serve you. Amen.

Pour children each a cup of clean water to drink while finishing their pretzels.

1 PETER

"You have not seen Christ, but still you love him. You cannot see him now, but you believe in him. So you are filled with a joy that cannot be explained, a joy full of glory."

1 Peter 1:8, NCV

1 PETER
1:22

THEME:

Love one another with all your heart.

SUMMARY:

Use this music idea to teach children that God wants us to love each other.

PREPARATION:

You'll need a Bible.

Open your Bible to 1 Peter 1:22, show children the passage, and read it aloud. Say: **That means that God wants us to love each other with all our hearts.**

Ask:

• **What do you think it means to love someone with all your heart?**

• **Why do you think God wants us to love each other?**

• **How can we show people that we love them?**

Lead children in the words and motions to the following song sung to the tune of "Mary Had a Little Lamb."

Jesus said love everyone *(hug a child)*,

Everyone, everyone. *(Point to other children.)*

Jesus said love everyone. *(Hug a child.)*

Love them from your heart. *(Point to heart then open arms wide.)*

Close in prayer, thanking God for loving us, and asking him to help us love others.

1 PETER
4:10

THEME:

Use your talents for God.

SUMMARY:

Use this field trip to teach children that they have a special gift they can share with others.

PREPARATION:

You'll need a Bible and other items as described below, based on activities your children choose.

Before this activity, contact a local children's shelter or orphanage to arrange a time for your class to visit. Then make arrangements for drivers and parent helpers. You'll need a permission form for each child.

Open your Bible to 1 Peter 4:10, show children the passage, and read it aloud. Say: **Each one of us has special gifts or talents that God has given us. God wants us to share those gifts with others.**

Ask:

• **What is one of your special gifts or talents?**

• **How do you think it would make other people feel if you shared those gifts with them? Why?**

• **How would you feel sharing your gifts with others? Why?**

Say: **We're going on a field trip to share our special gifts with other children.**

Before you leave on your field trip, help children decide what they want to do. Some may want to decorate prebaked cookies to deliver to the children. Others may want to draw pictures to give or perform a favorite song or rhyme. Have adult helpers assist children as they prepare for the trip. Remind children that each person is special with special gifts to share.

When you return from the field trip, thank the children for sharing their gifts and talents. Then close in prayer, thanking God for the talents he gives us.

1 PETER 5:7

THEME:
Give your worries to God.

SUMMARY:
Use this quiet reflection idea to teach children to pray when they're afraid.

PREPARATION:
You'll need a Bible.

Open your Bible to 1 Peter 5:7, show children the passage, and read it aloud. Say: **This means that we should give all our worries to God.**

Ask:

• **What does it mean to worry?**

Say: **Worries are things that we think a lot about or are afraid of. God doesn't want us to worry because he is always with us and will never leave us.**

Ask:

• **What's one thing you're afraid of?**

Say: **When you're afraid, you can pray to God to help you. Let's learn this prayer that we can say when we're afraid. It'll remind us that God is always with us.**

Teach children this rhyming

prayer. Then have children substitute other things they're afraid of in place of "When I'm in the dark." For example, a child might say, "When a dog barks" or "When I hear it thunder."

Dear God,

When I'm in the dark, and I have a fear,

Help me feel you standing here.

Amen.

2 PETER

"Grace and peace be yours in abundance through the knowledge of God and of Jesus our Lord."

2 Peter 1:2

2 PETER 1:3

THEME:

We can serve God.

SUMMARY:

Use this service idea to teach children that when we serve God, we help others.

PREPARATION:

You'll need a Bible and a beach ball.

Have children sit in a circle. Open your Bible to 2 Peter 1:3, show children the passage, and read it aloud. Say: **This means that Jesus' power gives us everything we need to love and serve God. When we serve God, we help other people.**

Ask:

• **Why does God want us to serve and help others?**

• **How does God feel when we help others?**

Talk about the different things we can do to serve God. For example, to help out at home, we can clean our rooms, pick up our toys, help take out the trash, or set the table. We can help our neighbors by sharing a special toy, sending a card to someone who is sick, or visiting a neighbor who is lonely. Ask:

• **How does it make you feel when you help someone?**

• **How do you feel when some-one helps you?**

Have children each think of one thing they can do during the week to help others and serve God. Say: **Let's play a game. We'll roll this beach ball around the circle as we sing a special song. When we get to the end of the song, if you're holding the ball, you have to say what you thought of that you'll do to serve God this week.** Teach children the following song to the tune of "This Old Man."

> **Help us, God, to serve you.**
> **We help others when we do.**
> **This week I'll serve you in a special way.**
> **This is what I'll do one day.**

Begin the song and roll the ball randomly around the circle. When the song ends, have the child holding the ball share how he or she will serve God. Continue singing the song and passing the ball until everyone has had a turn to share. If a child who has already had a turn ends up holding the ball at the end of the song, have that child roll the ball to another child who hasn't had a turn.

After each child has had a turn, close in prayer, asking God to help the children as they serve others with the special deeds they've chosen.

2 PETER 3:9

THEME:

God waits for us to repent.

SUMMARY:

Use this learning game to teach children that God waits for us to stop doing bad things and to do good things.

PREPARATION:

You'll need a Bible and a large, red paper octagon.

Have kids race across the room. Then have them do it again in slow motion. Ask:

• **Why did we run a slow race?**

Say: **People are often in a hurry, and the fastest people are the ones who win prizes. Today we're going to learn that sometimes slow is good.**

Ask:

• **How does it feel to wait for Christmas?**

Say: **It seems like Christmas will never come, and then finally it does. Well, there's something**

even better than Christmas that Christians are waiting for. It's the day that Jesus will come to earth again. And God is waiting too.

Ask:

• **What do you think God is waiting for?**

Say: **Let's look at what the Bible says.**

Open your Bible to 2 Peter 3:9, show children the passage, and read it aloud. Say: **God is waiting for more people to repent and follow him. To repent means to stop doing the bad things we've done, and do good things instead.**

Hold up the red octagon. Say: **Maybe you've seen a red sign like this while riding in a car.**

Ask:

• **What does this sign tell drivers to do?**

Have kids stand against a wall at one end of the room. Tell them to walk toward you until you hold up your sign, then they need to stop and turn and face the other direction. Move to the other end so you're in front of the children and repeat the action. After a few minutes of this game, say: **When we repent, we stop doing bad things. Then we need to turn around and start doing what's right.**

Have children follow these directions as you lead them in this prayer.

Dear God,

Thank you for waiting for me to repent.

Help me to stop *(hold out hand in front of self)*,

And turn around *(turn around and face the opposite direction)*,

And go the right way. *(Take one step forward.)*

Amen.

1 JOHN

"This is the confidence we have in approaching God: that if we ask anything according to his will, he hears us."

1 John 5:14

1 JOHN
4:7a

THEME:

Love comes from God.

SUMMARY:

Use this game to teach children that we can love others the way God loves us.

PREPARATION:

You'll need a Bible, masking tape, and a ball.

Before children arrive, use masking tape to make a large X in the middle of the playing area.

Gather children in a circle around the X, and say: **God loves us so much! The Bible even tells us that love comes from God.** Open your Bible to 1 John 4:7a, show children the passage, and read it aloud. **Let's show each other God's love by playing a hugging game called Hug-a-Bug.**

Toss the ball to a child who becomes the "Bug." The Bug takes the ball and stands on the X in the middle of the circle. Have the rest of the children yell: **Hug-a-Bug**, and go into the middle of the circle and hug the Bug. Have children move back out to the circle, and let the Bug toss the ball to another child, who becomes the new Bug. Continue the game until all children have had a chance to be the Bug.

Say: **Now that we've all been hugged, let's learn a song about God's love.** Toss the ball around the circle while you lead children in singing this song to the tune of "This Old Man."

> I love God.
> God loves me.
> That's the way it ought to be!
> God will give me love,
> And I'll pass it on to you!
> Won't you say you love God too?

Ask:

• **How does God show his love to you?**

• **How does God feel when we love others?**

• **What would it be like if everyone showed God's love?**

Encourage children to practice the Hug-a-Bug game with their friends and family as a way to let others feel God's love.

1 JOHN
4:9-10

THEME:

We are special to God.

SUMMARY:

Use this affirmation activity to teach children that we are so special to God that he sent his Son, Jesus, to save us.

PREPARATION:

You'll need a Bible, tape, and a construction paper ribbon for each child with the words "I Am special!" written on them.

Tape an "I am special!" construction paper ribbon to each child as he or she enters the room, and say: **You are special to God!**

Gather children together. Open your Bible to 1 John 4:9-10, show children the passage, and read it aloud. Say: **God sent his Son, Jesus, to earth because we are so special to him and he loves us so much.**

Play this game to celebrate each child's unique abilities. Have children join hands and walk in a circle as they sing this song to the tune of "The Farmer in the Dell."

> **God made you special,**
> **God made me special.**
> **Amazing and wonderful,**
> **Just look what you can do.**

Each time the song is sung, have a different child tell one of his or her talents and then move to the center of the circle for the remainder of the game. Continue singing until you're the only one left in the circle.

Close in prayer, thanking God that we are special to him and that he loves us.

2 JOHN

"It has given me great joy to find some of your children walking in the truth, just as the Father commanded us."

2 John 4

2 JOHN 5-6

THEME:

God tells us to walk in love.

SUMMARY:

Use this craft idea to teach children that God commands us to walk in love and obedience.

PREPARATION:

You'll need a Bible, old newspapers, a six-foot length of butcher paper or newsprint for each child, washable tempera paint, a pie tin, a dishpan of water, paper towels, and liquid soap.

Before the activity, pour washable tempera paint into a pie tin, and add a few drops of liquid soap for easy cleanup. Cover the work area on the floor with newspapers. Roll out a six-foot length of butcher paper or newsprint for each child.

Open your Bible to 2 John 5-6, show children the passage, and read it aloud. Say: **This means that God tells us to walk in love.**

Ask:

• **How can we show others that we love them?**

Say: **When we are kind to others and show them that we love them, we're walking in love. Let's make footprint posters. You can hang your poster in your room to remind you that God tells us to walk in love.**

Have children take off their shoes and socks, step into the pie tin, and walk across their papers. Let the posters dry. Help children rinse their feet and then dry them with paper towels.

3 JOHN

"I have no greater joy than to hear that my children are walking in the truth."

3 John 4

3 JOHN 11

THEME:

We should follow Jesus.

SUMMARY:

Use this game to teach children that we follow Jesus when we imitate what is right.

PREPARATION:

You'll need a Bible.

Gather children together and lead them in a game of Follow the Leader. After a few minutes of play, choose another child to help you as the leader. Tell the child that he or she can do things such as hop on one leg, jump up and down, or skip, but to do actions different from you.

Lead the children in another round of play. It'll be confusing for the children to try to follow both leaders at the same time. After a few minutes, have children sit in a circle. Ask:

• **What was it like trying to follow both leaders at the same time?**

• **How did you know which leader to follow?**

Open your Bible to 3 John 11, show children the passage, and read it aloud. Ask:

• **What do you think it means to imitate someone?**

Say: **When we imitate someone, that means that we follow that person and we do what they do. The Bible tells us that we are to follow Jesus. When we follow Jesus, we imitate or do things that are right. We aren't supposed to imitate or follow things that are wrong.**

Ask:

• **How can we follow Jesus every day?**

• **How does Jesus feel when we follow him? Why?**

If time allows, play more rounds of Follow the Leader and let children take turns as the leader.

JUDE

"God is strong and can help you not to fall. He can bring you before his glory without any wrong in you and can give you great joy."

Jude 24, NCV

JUDE 20

THEME:

We can pray to God.

SUMMARY:

Use this active prayer to teach older preschoolers that our love for God grows as we pray to him.

PREPARATION:

You'll need a Bible, clear plastic cups, marbles, narcissus bulbs, and water.

Open your Bible to Jude 20, show children the passage, and read it aloud. Ask:

• **Why does God want us to pray?**

• **What are some ways we can pray?**

Say: **There are many different ways we can pray. It makes God happy however we pray because we're showing him that we love to talk with him. When we pray it helps our love for God to grow. Let's learn a special planting prayer to show God that we love him.**

Teach children the following rhyming prayer:

God, thank you for your love for me.

I'll always love you, too.

Help my love for you to grow

In everything I do.

Amen.

Have children each fill a plastic cup about three-fourths full of marbles. Then place the bulb, round side down, on top of the marbles. Place a few marbles around the bulb to hold it upright. Have children each fill his or her cup with water until it reaches the base of the bulb while repeating the planting prayer.

Say: **Take your plant home and place it in a sunny window. Check it every day to make sure the water stays just at the base of the bulb. You may need to add a little water. Then you can say our special planting prayer that we learned. As you pray every day, your love for God will grow just like the bulb you planted will sprout and grow.**

REVELATION

"You are worthy, our Lord and God, to receive glory and honor and power, for you created all things, and by your will they were created and have their being."

Revelation 4:11

REVELATION 5:8b

THEME:
Our prayers rise to God in heaven.

SUMMARY:
Use this craft idea to teach children that in heaven there are golden bowls that hold the prayers of God's people.

PREPARATION:
You'll need a Bible, golden modeling dough as described below, a scented candle, and matches.

Before the activity, make the modeling dough by adding six tablespoons of cooking oil to four cups of boiling water. Set aside. Next mix together four packets of unsweetened orange powdered drink mix, five cups of flour, and one cup of salt. Then slowly add the water and oil mixture to the dry mixture. Knead the dough until completely blended. Allow to cool completely, and place in an airtight container.

Gather children together and have them smell the scented candle. Review fire and match safety with children. Then light the candle

and place it out of children's reach. Say: **We're going to let the candle burn while we do our art activity and see if we can smell the scent.**

Open your Bible to Revelation 5:8b, show children the passage, and read it aloud. Say: **We're going to make golden bowls like the ones in heaven that hold the prayers of God's people.**

Give each child a portion of the dough. Have children smell the dough and play with it for a few minutes. Show children how to roll the dough into a ball and press one thumb into the center of the ball without breaking through to the bottom. Show children how to gently press open the center and squeeze the sides all the way around to create a small bowl. As children make their bowls, ask:

• **Do we see prayers going to heaven?**

• **How do we know our prayers reach God in heaven?**

Have children smell the air with the candle scent. Ask:

• **How do you think the smell from the candle got here?**

Say: **We can't see smells because they're invisible. But they travel in the air as the air moves. Our prayers are like smells. When we pray, our words travel invisibly up to God in heaven, who hears us.**

Have children take their bowls home as a reminder that God hears our prayers as they rise to heaven.

REVELATION 7:9

THEME:
God loves people around the world.

SUMMARY:
Use this learning game to teach children God is everywhere and loves people from all over.

PREPARATION:
You'll need a Bible, masking tape, a ball, and a globe. For extra impact, bring in pictures of children from other countries who are dressed in native or traditional clothing to show to your children.

Before the game, make a large masking tape circle on the floor. If you have more than ten children, you may want to make two circles and provide a ball for each group.

Have children sit on the masking tape line with their legs crossed. Hold up the globe and say: **Look at this globe. It is a model of our world and shows all of the** places in the world. There are people who live in each part of the land that we see. Those people might look different from us. They might even speak differently than we do.

Set down the globe, and pick up the ball. Say: **Let's pretend that this ball is the world. We'll roll the ball around the circle. Remember to keep the ball on the floor as you roll it to a friend across the circle. As we roll the ball back and forth, let's sing "Jesus Loves the Little Children" to remember all the children around the world.** As children play, be sure that every child has a turn to roll the ball. After singing the song at least twice, hold the ball, and ask:

• **How many people are in the world?**

• **Which people does God love?**

Say: **God isn't just here in this room. God is everywhere. He loves people who live near us and people who live far away from us. There's a verse in the Bible that tells about lots of people gathering to praise God.**

Open your Bible to Revelation 7:9, show children the passage, and read it aloud. Say: **This verse tells us that people who worship God look differently, speak differently, and live in different places. But God knows and understands all** of them. **God is everywhere and loves people from all over.**

Close in prayer, thanking God that he is everywhere, and asking him to watch over your children and the children of the world.

REVELATION 8:4

THEME:

God hears our prayers

SUMMARY:

Use this prayer to help children imagine their prayers rising to God.

PREPARATION:

You'll need a Bible and a large uninflated balloon.

Open your Bible to Revelation 8:4, show children the passage, and read it aloud. Say: **We can imagine our prayers rising to God, just like in the Scripture verse. We'll use this balloon to help us see our prayers. Each time you say a prayer, I'll fill our balloon with air. When we fill our balloon, we'll send our prayers to heaven.**

Start with a sentence prayer and then blow a breath of air into the balloon. As each child adds a sentence prayer, blow into the balloon. When the balloon is full, hold the balloon over your head and let it go. All together, say: **Amen.**

Ask:

• **How does it feel knowing that God hears your prayers?**

• **How do you feel when you pray to God?**

• **How do you think God feels when you pray to him?**

REVELATION 19:9a

THEME:

God gives us good things.

SUMMARY:

Use this craft to teach children that God gives us many wonderful things because he loves us.

PREPARATION:

You'll need a Bible, a large bunch of grapes, three small packages of grape-flavored unsweetened powdered drink mix, three ounces of nontoxic unscented hair-styling gel, a four-ounce squeeze bottle, and old newspapers. For each child you'll also need a paint smock and a circle of white paper taped inside the bottom of a pie tin.

Before the activity, mix the three packages of drink mix with the three ounces of hair-styling gel in the squirt bottle. Shake vigorously. Cover the work area with newspapers. Make sure every child wears a paint smock since the drink mix stains.

Have children sit in a circle. Say: **Tell me about a wonderful party that you've been to.** Allow the children to share. Open your Bible to Revelation 19:9a, show children the passage, and read it aloud

Say: **This wedding feast will be the best party ever. One of the things that were at wedding feasts long ago were lots of grapes and wine.** Pass around the grapes and let children take and eat a few.

Ask:

• **What are things that God gives us now?**

• **Why do you think God gives us many wonderful things?**

Have children each put on a paint smock and move to the art area. Give them each a pie tin. Pass around the remaining grapes and let children each pick one grape to paint with. Place a dime-sized squirt of paint on each child's pie tin. Have children smell the paint, but instruct them not to taste it. Then have children each place the grape inside the pie tin, carefully rolling it around through the paint to create a picture. Remove the grapes and allow the pictures to dry. Have children take home their pictures to remind them of all the wonderful things God gives us.

INDEXES

NEW TESTAMENT SCRIPTURE INDEX

Matthew 2:9-11   8
Matthew 2:11b   8
Matthew 3:16-17   9
Matthew 4:18-22   10
Matthew 5:16   10
Matthew 6:9-13   11
Matthew 6:28b   13
Matthew 8:23-27   14
Matthew 10:29-31   15
Matthew 14:13-21   16
Matthew 14:22-32   17
Matthew 16:17-18   18
Matthew 18:20   19
Matthew 19:13-15   20
Matthew 19:19b   20
Matthew 21:6-11   21
Matthew 25:35, 40   23
Matthew 26:14-16, 47-50   24
Matthew 27:45-56   24
Matthew 28:19a   25

Mark 1:3   28
Mark 1:12-13   28
Mark 1:16-18   29
Mark 2:1-12   30
Mark 4:1-20   31
Mark 4:21-23   32
Mark 4:30-32   33
Mark 4:36-41   34
Mark 5:27-28   35
Mark 6:30-44   36
Mark 6:45-51   38
Mark 10:13-16   39
Mark 10:46-52   39
Mark 12:28-31   41
Mark 14:32-42   41
Mark 14:66-72   42
Mark 15:33-39   43
Mark 15:33–16:20   44
Mark 16:1-6, 19   45
Mark 16:2-4   46

Luke 1:26-33   50
Luke 1:37   50

Luke 2:1-7   51
Luke 2:1-20   53
Luke 2:10   54
Luke 2:11   55
Luke 2:41-52   56
Luke 3:11   58
Luke 4:8b   59
Luke 6:38   61
Luke 8:5-8   63
Luke 8:22-25   64
Luke 10:25-37   65
Luke 10:38-42   66
Luke 11:1-4   67
Luke 12:48b   68
Luke 15:1-7   69
Luke 15:8-10   70
Luke 19:1-10   72
Luke 24:1-12   72

John 1:1-4, 14   76
John 1:43-51   76
John 2:1-11   77
John 2:13-22   78
John 3:12-21   79
John 3:16   80
John 4:1-30   81
John 5:1-18   82
John 6:1-13   83
John 6:5-15   84
John 9:1-12   85
John 10:14   86
John 10:27   86
John 11:25   87
John 11:35   88
John 13:2-17   89
John 13:34   90
John 14:6   91
John 15:1-5   92
John 21:4-17   93

Acts 2:1-21   96
Acts 2:44-45   97
Acts 3:1-8   99
Acts 9:23-25   100

Acts 9:26-28   101
Acts 14:17   101
Acts 16:22-28   102
Acts 17:24   103

Romans 1:16a   106
Romans 1:20a   106
Romans 2:11   107
Romans 5:8   109
Romans 6:6-7   109
Romans 6:23   110
Romans 8:38-39   111
Romans 12:6a   112

1 Corinthians 10:13b   116
1 Corinthians 12:17   116
1 Corinthians 13:4   118
1 Corinthians 14:15   119
1 Corinthians 15:58   120

2 Corinthians 2:14   122
2 Corinthians 3:18   123
2 Corinthians 5:17   124
2 Corinthians 8:7   125
2 Corinthians 9:7   127

Galatians 5:22-23   130
Galatians 6:9   131

Ephesians 4:32   134
Ephesians 5:8-9   135
Ephesians 6:16   135

Philippians 2:19-23   138
Philippians 4:14, 16   138

Colossians 1:16   142
Colossians 3:12   143

1 Thessalonians 1:4   146
1 Thessalonians 5:21   146

2 Thessalonians 2:13   150

1 Timothy 1:14   152
1 Timothy 2:1   153

2 Timothy 3:16-17   156
2 Timothy 4:2   157

Titus 3:5a   160

Philemon 4   162

Hebrews 3:13   164
Hebrews 4:12a   164
Hebrews 11:1   165
Hebrews 11:6   166
Hebrews 13:5b-6a   167
Hebrews 13:15   168

James 1:5   170
James 1:17a   171
James 2:8   172
James 5:13   172
James 5:16   173

1 Peter 1:22   176
1 Peter 4:10   176
1 Peter 5:7   177

2 Peter 1:3   180
2 Peter 3:9   181

1 John 4:7a   184
1 John 4:9-10   185

2 John 5-6   188

3 John 11   190

Jude 20   192

Revelation 5:8b   194
Revelation 7:9   195
Revelation 8:4   196
Revelation 19:9a   196

NEW TESTAMENT TEACHING-STYLE INDEX

AFFIRMATION ACTIVITIES

Matthew 3:16-17   9
Matthew 16:17-18   18
Mark 4:30-32   33
Mark 10:13-16   39
Luke 1:26-33   50
Luke 2:11   55
Luke 12:48b   68
Romans 12:6a   112
Ephesians 5:8-9   135
1 John 4:9-10   185

CRAFTS AND MAKABLES

Matthew 2:11b   8
Matthew 6:28b   13
Matthew 8:23-27   14
Matthew 10:29-31   15
Mark 6:30-44   36
Mark 16:2-4   46
Luke 2:10   54
John 2:1-11   77
John 10:27   86
Acts 2:1-21   96
Acts 14:17   101
Romans 6:6-7   109
1 Corinthians 12:17   116
Ephesians 6:16   135
2 Timothy 4:2   157
James 1:17a   171
2 John 5-6   188
Revelation 5:8b   194
Revelation 19:9a   196

CREATIVE STORYTELLING

Matthew 14:13-21   16
Matthew 14:22-32   17
Mark 4:1-20   31
Mark 10:46-52   39
Mark 15:33–16:20   44
Luke 2:41-52   56
Luke 8:22-25   64
Luke 15:1-7   69
John 2:13-22   78
John 4:1-30   81
John 6:1-13   83
John 21:4-17   93

DEVOTIONS

Matthew 18:20   19
Matthew 28:19a   25
Mark 5:27-28   35
Luke 3:11   58
Luke 4:8b   59
Luke 19:1-10   72
John 13:34   90
Romans 1:20a   106
Romans 6:23   110
1 Corinthians 13:4   118
1 Corinthians 15:58   120
2 Corinthians 5:17   124
Colossians 1:16   142
2 Timothy 3:16-17   156
Hebrews 4:12a   164
James 1:5   170

LEARNING GAMES

Mark 2:1-12   30
Mark 4:36-41   34
Mark 14:66-72   42
John 1:43-51   76
John 3:12-21   79
Acts 16:22-28   102
1 Corinthians 10:13b   116
Philippians 2:19-23   138
2 Thessalonians 2:13   150
Titus 3:5a   160
Hebrews 3:13   164
Hebrews 13:5b-6a   167
2 Peter 3:9   181
1 John 4:7a   184
3 John 11   190
Revelation 7:9   195

MUSIC AND FINGER PLAY IDEAS

Matthew 2:9-11   8
Matthew 4:18-22   10
Matthew 19:13-15   20
Matthew 27:45-56   24
Mark 1:12-13   28
Mark 12:28-31   41
Mark 15:33-39   43
Mark 16:1-6, 19   45
Luke 10:38-42   66
John 1:1-4, 14   76
John 6:5-15   84
Acts 9:23-25   100
Acts 9:26-28   101
Acts 17:24   103
Romans 1:16a   106
2 Corinthians 9:7   127
Galatians 5:22-23   130
Ephesians 4:32   134
Hebrews 11:1   165
James 2:8   172
1 Peter 1:22   176

OBJECT LESSONS

Mark 1:3   28
Mark 4:21-23   32
Luke 1:37   50
Luke 2:1-20   53
Luke 8:5-8   63
Luke 15:8-10   70
John 5:1-18   82
John 10:14   86
John 11:25   87
John 14:6   91
Romans 2:11   107
Romans 5:8   109
2 Corinthians 2:14   122
2 Corinthians 3:18   123
Galatians 6:9   131
1 Thessalonians 5:21   146
1 Timothy 1:14   152
Hebrews 11:6   166
James 5:16   173

PARTIES

Matthew 21:6-11   21
Mark 1:16-18   29
Luke 2:1-7   51
Luke 24:1-12   72

PRAYERS AND QUIET REFLECTIONS

Matthew 6:9-13   11
Matthew 19:19b   20
Matthew 25:35, 40   23
Matthew 26:14-16, 47-50   24
Mark 6:45-51   38
Mark 14:32-42   41
Luke 11:1-4   67
John 3:16   80
John 9:1-12   85
John 11:35   88
John 15:1-5   92
1 Thessalonians 1:4   146
1 Timothy 2:1   153
Philemon 4   162
Hebrews 13:15   168
James 5:13   172
1 Peter 5:7   177
Jude 20   192
Revelation 8:4   196

SERVICE PROJECTS AND MISSIONS

Matthew 5:16   10
Luke 6:38   61
Luke 10:25-37   65
John 13:2-17   89
Acts 2:44-45   97
2 Corinthians 8:7   125
Philippians 4:14, 16   138
2 Peter 1:3   180

TRIPS 'N' TRAVELS

Acts 3:1-8   99
Romans 8:38-39   111
1 Corinthians 14:15   119
Colossians 3:12   143
1 Peter 4:10   176

NEW TESTAMENT THEME INDEX

BIBLE

It's important to hear God's Word and learn
   from it (Mark 4:1-20). 31
The Bible is our instruction book
   (2 Timothy 3:16-17). 156
The Bible is God's living Word
   (Hebrews 4:12a). 164

CREATION

God made all things in creation
   (Matthew 6:28b). 13
God made everything (Acts 17:24). 103
God wants us to enjoy all the great things
   he made (Colossians 1:16). 142

FAITH

Let your faith in Jesus shine
   (Mark 4:21-23). 32
Keep your eyes on Jesus (Mark 6:45-51). 38
We can trust Jesus to help us
   (Luke 8:22-25). 64
We need Jesus to help us grow
   (John 15:1-5). 92
God is invisible, yet we know he exists
   (Romans 1:20a). 106
Jesus makes us new
   (2 Corinthians 5:17). 124
I believe in Jesus (Hebrews 11:1). 165
We believe in God (Hebrews 11:6). 166

FAITHFULNESS

God wants us to please him
   (Matthew 3:16-17). 9
We need Jesus to help us grow
   (John 15:1-5). 92
God is faithful in providing for our needs
   (Acts 14:17). 101
God never turns away from us
   (1 Corinthians 10:13b). 116

FORGIVENESS

Jesus wants us to forgive others
   (Mark 14:66-72). 42
Jesus forgives our sins (John 21:4-17). 93
God forgives our sins (Romans 6:6-7). 109

FRIENDS & NEIGHBORS

Jesus wants us to love others
   (Matthew 19:19b). 20
God wants us to share with others
   (Matthew 25:35, 40). 23
Jesus wants us to be a good friend to others
   (Matthew 26:14-16, 47-50). 24
We can love God and our neighbors
   (Mark 12:28-31). 41
Jesus wants us to forgive others
   (Mark 14:66-72). 42
Share with your neighbors (Luke 3:11). 58
God wants us to help our neighbors
   (Luke 10:25-37). 65
Jesus wants us to serve others
   (John 13:2-17). 89
Help others as you are able (Acts 3:1-8). 99
God wants us to help others
   (Acts 9:23-25). 100
God wants us to share Jesus' love with
   others (2 Corinthians 2:14). 122
Be happy when you share with others
   (2 Corinthians 9:7). 127
Do not grow weary (Galatians 6:9). 131
God wants us to be good friends
   (Philippians 2:19-23). 138
God wants us to help those in need
   (Philippians 4:14, 16). 138
God wants us to care for others
   (Colossians 3:12). 143
We can pray for others (1 Timothy 2:1). 153
Pray for each other (Philemon 4). 162
Love your neighbors (James 2:8). 172
Love one another with all your heart
   (1 Peter 1:22). 176

GIFTS

The wise men bring gifts
   (Matthew 2:9-11). 8
We can give gifts to Jesus
   (Matthew 2:11b). 8
Jesus is the greatest gift of all
   (Luke 2:1-7). 51
God sent his Son (Luke 2:1-20). 53
You are Jesus' treasure (Luke 15:8-10). 70

Jesus is the greatest gift (John 3:16). 80
God gives us eternal life (Romans 6:23). 110
We can give good gifts to God
(1 Corinthians 15:58). 120
Good gifts come from God
(James 1:17a). 171

GIVING
We can give gifts to Jesus
(Matthew 2:11b). 8
God loves a cheerful giver (Luke 6:38). 61
God wants us to give to others
(Acts 2:44-45). 97
We can give good gifts to God
(1 Corinthians 15:58). 120
God wants us to give generously
(2 Corinthians 8:7). 125

GOD'S CARE
God cares for us (Matthew 10:29-31; Luke
15:1-7). 15, 69
God is always with us (Matthew 18:20). 19
We're part of God's kingdom
(Mark 4:30-32). 33
God provides for all our needs
(Mark 6:30-44; John 6:5-15). 36
God sent his Son (Luke 2:1-20). 53, 84
We can reach out to God (John 5:1-18). 82
God is faithful in providing for our needs
(Acts 14:17). 101
God is always with us (Romans 8:38-39;
Ephesians 6:16; Hebrews 13:5b-6a). 111,
135, 167
God never turns away from us
(1 Corinthians 10:13b). 116
God wants us to enjoy all the great things
he made (Colossians 1:16). 142
God gives us wisdom (James 1:5). 170
Give your worries to God (1 Peter 5:7). 177
God waits for us to repent (2 Peter 3:9). 181
God gives us good things
(Revelation 19:9a). 196

GOD'S GIFTS
God sent his Son (Luke 2:1-20). 53
God gives us different talents and gifts
(Luke 12:48b). 68
Jesus is the greatest gift (John 3:16). 80

God gave us the Holy Spirit
(Acts 2:1-21). 96
God gives us eternal life (Romans 6:23). 110
God gives us fruits of the Spirit
(Galatians 5:22-23). 130
God pours out his grace on us
(1 Timothy 1:14). 152
Good gifts come from God
(James 1:17a). 171

GOD'S LOVE
We are special to God
(Matthew 16:17-18). 18
We're part of God's kingdom
(Mark 4:30-32). 33
God sent his Son (Luke 2:1-20). 53
Jesus came to let us be a part of God's
family (Luke 2:11). 55
God's love grows in our hearts
(Luke 8:5-8). 63
We can reach out to God (John 5:1-18). 82
We're all God's favorites (Romans 2:11). 107
God forgives our sins (Romans 6:6-7). 109
God made me special (Romans 12:6a). 112
We are special to God
(1 Corinthians 12:17; 1 John 4:9-10). 116,
185
We are transformed by God
(2 Corinthians 3:18). 123
We are chosen by God
(1 Thessalonians 1:4). 146
We are set apart for God
(2 Thessalonians 2:13). 150
God pours out his grace on us
(1 Timothy 1:14). 152
We can share the good news of God's love
(2 Timothy 4:2). 157
God waits for us to repent (2 Peter 3:9). 181
Love comes from God (1 John 4:7a). 184
God loves people around the world
(Revelation 7:9). 195

GOD'S POWER
God made all things in creation
(Matthew 6:28b). 13
God is always with us (Matthew 18:20;
Romans 8:38-39; Ephesians 6:16). 19,
111, 135

God can do anything (Luke 1:37). 50
God knows everything about you
(John 1:43-51). 76
God can work miracles (John 2:1-11). 77
God made everything (Acts 17:24). 103
God is invisible, yet we know he exists
(Romans 1:20a). 106
We are transformed by God
(2 Corinthians 3:18). 123
God wants us to enjoy all the great things
he made (Colossians 1:16). 142
God gives us wisdom (James 1:5). 170

GOSPEL
We can share the good news
(Matthew 28:19a). 25
We can share the good news of Jesus
(Luke 2:10). 54
Jesus is the way (John 14:6). 91
We can share the good news of God's love
(2 Timothy 4:2). 157

JESUS' CARE
Jesus helps us (Matthew 14:22-32). 17
Jesus comforts us (Mark 5:27-28). 35
Jesus came to let us be a part of God's
family (Luke 2:11). 55
Jesus teaches us to pray (Luke 11:1-4). 67
Jesus is the light of the world
(John 1:1-4, 14). 76
Jesus can heal the wounds of our world
(John 9:1-12). 85
We are Jesus' sheep (John 10:27). 86
Jesus understands our feelings
(John 11:35). 88
Jesus is the way (John 14:6). 91
We need Jesus to help us grow
(John 15:1-5). 92
Jesus makes us new
(2 Corinthians 5:17). 124

JESUS' LOVE
Jesus loves children (Matthew 19:13-15). 20
Jesus died for us because he loves us
(Matthew 27:45-56; Mark 15:33-39;
Romans 5:8). 24, 43, 109
You are important to Jesus
(Mark 10:13-16). 39

Jesus loves me (Luke 1:26-33). 50
We can share the good news of Jesus
(Luke 2:10). 54
You are Jesus' treasure (Luke 15:8-10). 70
Jesus loves everyone (Luke 19:1-10). 72
Jesus came to save us (John 3:12-21). 79
Jesus' love is for everyone (John 4:1-30). 81
Our heavenly identity comes from Jesus
(John 10:14). 86
Jesus' love never runs out (John 11:25). 87
God wants us to share Jesus' love with
others (2 Corinthians 2:14).122
Jesus makes us new
(2 Corinthians 5:17). 124

JESUS' POWER
Jesus is more powerful than anything
(Matthew 8:23-27). 14
Jesus heals (Mark 2:1-12). 30
Jesus performs many miracles
(Matthew 14:13-21; Mark 4:36-41,
10:46-52). 34
Jesus is alive (Mark 15:33–16:20; Luke
24:1-12). 44
Jesus has risen (Mark 16:2-4). 46
Jesus is risen (Mark 16:1-6, 19). 45
Jesus grows wise (Luke 2:41-52). 56
Jesus is the light of the world
(John 1:1-4, 14). 76
Jesus can heal the wounds of our world
(John 9:1-12). 85
Jesus' love never runs out (John 11:25). 87
Jesus makes us new
(2 Corinthians 5:17). 124

LOVE
Jesus loves children (Matthew 19:13-15). 20
Jesus wants us to love others
(Matthew 19:19b). 20
Jesus died for us because he loves us
(Matthew 27:45-56). 24
We can love God and our neighbors
(Mark 12:28-31). 41
Jesus loves me (Luke 1:26-33). 50
God's love grows in our hearts
(Luke 8:5-8). 63
Jesus loves everyone (Luke 19:1-10). 72
Jesus' love is for everyone (John 4:1-30). 81

Jesus' love never runs out (John 11:25). 87
God commands us to love others
(John 13:34). 90
Love is not envious (1 Corinthians 13:4). 118
God wants us to share Jesus' love with
others (2 Corinthians 2:14). 122
Love your neighbors (James 2:8). 172
Love one another with all your heart
(1 Peter 1:22). 176
Love comes from God (1 John 4:7a). 184
God tells us to walk in love (2 John 5-6). 188
God loves people around the world
(Revelation 7:9). 195

MIRACLES
Jesus heals (Mark 2:1-12). 30
Jesus performs many miracles
(Matthew 14:13-21; Mark 4:36-41;
10:46-52). 16, 34, 39
God can work miracles (John 2:1-11). 77

PRAISE & WORSHIP
We can praise Jesus (Matthew 21:6-11). 21
We must worship God only
(Mark 1:12-13). 28
We're created to worship God
(Luke 4:8b). 59
Worship is important to God
(John 2:13-22). 78
Praise God in all things (Acts 16:22-28). 102
We can praise God (Hebrews 13:15). 168
Sing praises to God (James 5:13). 172

PRAYER
We should pray to God
(Matthew 6:9-13). 11
Jesus wants us to pray (Mark 14:32-42). 41
Jesus teaches us to pray (Luke 11:1-4). 67
We can pray for others (1 Timothy 2:1). 153
Pray for each other (Philemon 4). 162
We can pray to God (Jude 20). 192
Our prayers rise to God in heaven
(Revelation 5:8b). 194
God hears our prayers (Revelation 8:4). 196

SALVATION
Jesus died for us (Mark 15:33-39;
Romans 5:8). 43, 109

Jesus came to save us (John 3:12-21).79
Jesus is the way (John 14:6). 91
God gives us eternal life (Romans 6:23). 110
Jesus saves us (Titus 3:5a). 160

SERVING GOD
God wants us to please him
(Matthew 3:16-17). 9
We should pray to God
(Matthew 6:9-13). 11
We must worship God only
(Mark 1:12-13). 28
Jesus grows wise (Luke 2:41-52). 56
We're created to worship God
(Luke 4:8b). 59
God wants us to help our neighbors
(Luke 10:25-37). 65
Worship is important to God
(John 2:13-22). 78
God commands us to love others
(John 13:34). 90
God wants us to give to others
(Acts 2:44-45). 97
Praise God in all things (Acts 16:22-28). 102
God wants us to spend time with him
(1 Corinthians 14:15). 119
God wants us to share Jesus' love with
others (2 Corinthians 2:14). 122
God wants us to give generously
(2 Corinthians 8:7). 125
Be happy when you share with others
(2 Corinthians 9:7). 127
Do not grow weary (Galatians 6:9). 131
Be kind to other people
(Ephesians 4:32). 134
God wants us to test all things
(1 Thessalonians 5:21). 146
We are set apart for God
(2 Thessalonians 2:13). 150
We can praise God (Hebrews 13:15). 168
Sing praises to God (James 5:13). 172
God wants us to confess our sins
(James 5:16). 173
Use your talents for God (1 Peter 4:10). 176
We can serve God (2 Peter 1:3). 180
God waits for us to repent (2 Peter 3:9). 181
God tells us to walk in love (2 John 5-6). 188

SERVING JESUS

We can follow Jesus (Matthew 4:18-22). 10

Shine your light for Jesus
(Matthew 5:16). 10

Jesus wants us to love others
(Matthew 19:19b). 20

We can praise Jesus (Matthew 21:6-11). 21

We can prepare our hearts for Jesus
(Mark 1:3). 28

Jesus wants us to follow him
(Mark 1:16-18). 29

Jesus wants us to spend time with him
(Luke 10:38-42). 66

Jesus wants us to share (John 6:1-13). 83

Jesus wants us to serve others
(John 13:2-17). 89

Turn your life around and follow Jesus
(Acts 9:26-28). 101

We are proud to follow Jesus
(Romans 1:16a). 106

Let your light for Jesus shine through
(Ephesians 5:8-9). 135

We should follow Jesus (3 John 11). 190

SERVING OTHERS

God wants us to share with others
(Matthew 25:35, 40). 23

Jesus wants us to be a good friend to others
(Matthew 26:14-16, 47-50). 24

We can share the good news of Jesus
(Matthew 28:19a; Luke 2:10). 25, 54

God wants us to help our neighbors
(Luke 10:25-37). 65

Jesus wants us to serve others
(John 13:2-17). 89

God wants us to give to others
(Acts 2:44-45). 97

Help others as you are able
(Acts 3:1-8). 99

God wants us to help others
(Acts 9:23-25). 100

Be happy when you share with others
(2 Corinthians 9:7). 127

Be kind to other people
(Ephesians 4:32). 134

Let your light for Jesus shine through
(Ephesians 5:8-9). 135

God wants us to help those in need
(Philippians 4:14, 16). 138

God wants us to care for others
(Colossians 3:12). 143

We can share the good news of God's love
(2 Timothy 4:2). 157

God wants us to encourage others
(Hebrews 3:13). 164

SIN

God forgives our sins (Romans 6:6-7). 109

God wants us to confess our sins
(James 5:16). 173

God waits for us to repent (2 Peter 3:9). 181

TRUST

God is always with us (Matthew 18:20;
Romans 8:38-39; Ephesians 6:16;
Hebrews 13:5b-6a). 19, 111, 135, 167

We can trust Jesus to help us
(Luke 8:22-25). 64

God provides for our needs
(John 6:5-15). 84

God is faithful in providing for our needs
(Acts 14:17). 101

God never turns away from us
(1 Corinthians 10:13b). 116

Give your worries to God (1 Peter 5:7). 178

God gives us good things
(Revelation 19:9a). 196